R.E.N.E.W.

Removing **E**very **N**egative **E**motion & **W**ord

IT'S TIME TO CLOSE THE COMMUNICATION GAP

Marquis Cooper, Sr. M.Ed (ABD) & Tina Duffy

Foreword by: Dr. Marilyn Bailey

authorHOUSE®

AuthorHouse™
1663 Liberty Drive
Bloomington, IN 47403
www.authorhouse.com
Phone: 1-800-839-8640

Published by AuthorHouse 8/14/2012

ISBN: 978-1-4772-5372-4 (sc)
ISBN: 978-1-4772-5370-0 (e)

Library of Congress Control Number: 2012913491

What teenagers, educators, and parents are saying about R.E.N.E.W.

"The R.E.N.E.W. curriculum is so powerful that one cannot read through the curriculum without doing some self reflection. I challenge ALL people in leadership roles to utilize the RENEW curriculum and witness the difference it can make within their organization."- **Jessica Foreman- Baker Elementary 5th grade teacher- Pulaski County Special School District**

"This curriculum breaks down your thought process. I think it can be very beneficial to adults and educators as well. I really enjoyed it and I'm certain you will too."- **Breia Patterson- Maumelle High School**

"My attitude has gotten a lot better. I am maturing more each day thinking of what I learned in this R.E.N.E.W. program."- **Chastity Moore- Maumelle High School**

"I was very hard headed when I started the R.E.N.E.W. curriculum, but now all my grades are no lower than B's and my behavior is a lot better. This curriculum helps people change for the better not the worse."- **Jamal Nwachuku- Maumelle High School**

"The R.E.N.E.W. curriculum will change lives! It motivates one to believe that their imagination for their future, must be greater than the memories of their past. I wish this curriculum was available to me when I was a teenager. It would have changed my life and my choices tremendously." - **Claudette W. Holt, MS- Conway, AR**

"It has helped me a lot with my behavior, how I act towards others and my grades are a lot better. The R.E.N.E.W. sessions have really helped me a lot."- **Brittany Thompson- Maumelle High School**

"Before I started R.E.N.E.W. Dyamond was Dyamond meaning I said what I felt whether it hurt others or not. Now I take my time, step back, breathe and say ok."- **Dyamond Stephenson- Maumelle High School**

"The R.E.N.E.W. group has had a very powerful impact on me not just with school but with life itself."- **Tiana Tucker- Maumelle High School**

"I think anyone could benefit from this program because it teaches you what you think you already know that you really don't know."- **Marcia Daniels- Maumelle High School**

"The curriculum teaches you not only how to stay focused in school, but also how to stay focused in life."- **Tyshun Robinson- Maumelle High School**

"The R.E.N.E.W. curriculum will be an essential tool for all clinicians to utilize with adolescents in their practice. This tool will assist the adolescent population with connecting their emotions with their behaviors. It will also give them a better understanding of why they do what they do."

Freda Thomas, LCSW, CART- Private Practitioner- Texarkana, AR

"I saw myself as being useless to my parents. Now I wake up, work, and do the best I can each and every day."- **Moesha Smith- Maumelle High School**

"I really learned a lot about relationships. It helped me understand that I didn't need all that and I don't deserve to get treated like that."- **Analilia Atilano- Maumelle High School**

"Being a part of R.E.N.E.W. allowed me to take back control of my life."- **Nad'Deka Mays- Maumelle High School**

"I get along with my family better and I've become a better person. I finally realized who I am and how I need to be."- **Kirsten Farnam- Maumelle High School**

"When I first started I thought I knew it all but then I started listening. I've learned a lot of valuable life lessons."- **Paige Smith- Maumelle High School**

"I am truly inspired to help create positive change within our children."- **Sonja Hopkins-Hubbard- Crystal Hill Elementary Home School Counselor- Pulaski County School District**

"R.E.N.E.W. has given me time to be inspired and to think about my grades. I've learned how to deal with certain family issues a lot better."- **John Henry- Maumelle High School**

"Before I started the R.E.N.E.W. group I was doing bad at everything but now I'm doing everything I need to."- **Kennedy Robinson- Maumelle High School**

"I have started to focus more on my work. I learned how important it is for me to be successful."- **Sidney McCoy- Maumelle High School**

"My attitude is a lot better and my grades have improved."- **Trevor Johnese- Maumelle High School**

"I saw myself as a good person but off track, but now I'm a better person that's on track. I still struggle from time to time but I'm a lot better."- **Kevin Williamson- Maumelle High School**

"Before I saw myself not passing, not trying in school, and now I see myself doing better and being prepared for next school year."- **Tati-Yana Williams- Maumelle High School**

"It made me a better person."- **Domonique Hobson- Maumelle High School**

"My attitude has been a lot better since being a part of the R.E.N.E.W. group."- **Andrea Bunting- Maumelle High School**

Table of Contents

Acknowledgements

First and foremost I want to thank God for giving me the vision to write this curriculum at such a time as this. I want to thank the greatest individuals in my life, my wife Karmen Parker Cooper, my wonderful children Marquis and Cobie Cooper, and ALL my students (my other sons and daughters). I want to thank my parents who instilled in me the courage to finish what I started. I know you're no longer with me physically, but the values you instilled in me will live forever. I want to thank all of my brothers and sisters (all18), my good friends Tiffany Wright and Tamika Washington, and all the supportive people that believed this curriculum would help to change the lives of teenagers, educators, and parents across the country. I want to thank my mentors Mrs. Virginia Abrams and Gene Elms for always believing in me. I want to thank Sheryl Alexander and the teenagers at Greater Center Star M.B. Church. I want to thank the administrative staff and the entire 9th grade PLC team (especially Mrs. Lori Lachowsky) at Maumelle High School. I also want to thank the 2011-2012 9th grade students at Maumelle High School for being the first group of high school students to experience the entire curriculum. You guys have really inspired me to keep making a difference in the lives of other youth in the state of Arkansas and across the nation. Thanks for being the first groups of teenagers to believe in this God given mandate.

A special thank you goes out to my 5th grade teacher Mrs. Bobbie Banks and my high school counselor Mr. Michael Rodriguez. Thanks for helping me unlock my gift early on in life. You two were amazing then and you are still amazing now!!!!

Foreword

With wisdom beyond his years, Marquis Cooper demonstrates himself to be a keen visionary imparting knowledge to restore a broken nation. The author provides insightful knowledge that can be used to align the relationship between parents and their children and mothers and fathers—those engaged, married, or divorced. Young women and single mothers can find the answer to why there is such disappointment in the struggle to find a man to love, while gaining some clarity on the rules of engagement in a fatherless household. Through the articulation of "when the man is out of place, the woman becomes displaced, and the children become misplaced", the author speaks truths that reveal the concomitant milieu of events that occur in many diverse and homogenous communities. Yes, the message resonates with the black community; however, it is irrespective of person or nationality.

The reader will get a historical perspective on the cause and effect of relationships influx. Through the significance of an unopened letter written over 300 years ago, the reader will explore behavioral implications that have gone unaccounted for until now. The letter reveals a plan that has influenced the demise of a race of people. But, what is so phenomenal to me is that the strategy for survival is revealed through the poignant writings and questions of these remarkable authors.

I believe this companion workbook serves as a valuable tool for self-assessment and documenting personal strengths and limitations, while being a guide for opening dialogue that leads to the building of healthy relationships and sustainable change within the family unit. Such dialogue will uncover common myths that speak meaning into our lives. So read on and let your life be magnified to a state of joyful uplifting as you bask in a river of knowledge that empowers the soul!

Marilyn Walters Bailey, Ed. D

Suggestions for Using This Manual

I. HELPFUL MATERIALS

1. A copy of the book (optional). If you don't use the book the timeline found on the next page will still be the same just without the use of the book.
2. Internet access (for you to research information that you may need clarity on).
3. A mechanical pencil. Don't use ink because you may want to change your answers as you go through the workbook.
4. A journal or notebook to jot down other thoughts you may have as you read.

II. HINTS FOR PERSONAL STUDY

1. Remove all distractions (all forms of social media) as you prepare to begin a journey for change.
2. Don't worry about what you don't understand. Simply concentrate on the questions that you can answer. Go back and reread the material in the book to help clarify things you need help with.
3. Feel free to highlight things that stand out to you as you read the book and workbook.
4. Read each chapter (optional) until the chapter becomes a part of you.

III. HOW TO GET THE MOST OUT OF YOUR CLASS TIME

1. Attend every class period.
2. Read the chapter (optional) and answer the questions in the workbook PRIOR to attending class.
3. Have follow up questions already written down in your personal notebook (optional).
4. Write down things you want to remember.
5. Be a willing participant in the class discussions.

IV. HOW TO ANSWER THE QUESTIONS IN THE CURRICULUM

1. Be sure to follow the guidelines in the workbook. They will help you to stay on track with your journey.
2. Be honest and truthful with yourself as you answer the questions.
3. Share your experience of growth with others once you complete the journey.

Suggested Timeline
(With or WOut the Book)

Week 1-Getting started with R.E.N.E.W.

- 1). Read and discuss pages xv-xviii in the workbook with the entire class. 2). Allow students an opportunity to complete the short questionnaire on pages 1 & 2. 3). Have the students to write a short paragraph on what they think the book will be about based on the title.

Week 2- Damaged House (Students will spend time analyzing idle sayings and the true origin of those words).

- Class: 1) Discuss chapter one definitions in the workbook, complete pages 1 & 2 in the workbook prior to reading pages 1-6 in the book. 2).Complete page 4 in the workbook after reading page 6.

- Homework: 1).Read the remainder of Chapter 1 and answer the questions on page 10 in the book. 2).Complete pages 5-7 in the workbook.

Week 3- Unopened Letter (Students will explore the William Lynch letter of 1712, in an effort to shift the axis on the principles that have framed the thought process of African Americans for years).

- Class: 1).Discuss results from the questionnaire (See Appendix A on A on pages 91 - 92 for ways to share). 2).Complete pages 11-12 in the workbook before reading pages 11-15 in the book. 3). Complete page 14 in the workbook and discuss letter 1.

- Homework: Read pages 16-18 in the book and complete pages 15-16 in the workbook.

Week 4- Unopened Letter (Cont'd) (Students will explore the William Lynch letter of 1712, in an effort to shift the axis on the principles that have framed the thought process of African Americans for years).

- Class: Discuss chapter three definitions in the workbook, complete pages 20-21 in the workbook, and read pages 21-25 in the book.

- Homework: Read pages 26-31in the book and complete page 22 in the workbook.

Week 5-Name Search (Students will learn the true value of their names and begin to apply that meaning on a daily basis).

- Class: Discuss chapter 4 definitions in the workbook, read pages 33-36 in the book, and complete page 29 in the workbook. Invite guest speaker to talk to the males for the first 30 minutes of class. Females will complete page 30 and have discussion with female group leader for the first 30 minutes of class. Bring both genders back together for last half of class to talk.

- Homework: Write a paragraph on why you feel it's easier to communicate without the opposite gender being present?

Week 6-Purpose vs. Appointment (Students will learn the traits and qualities of both the Bruh and the Male).

- Class: Review chapter 4 definitions, read pages 36-38 in the book, and complete page 32 in the workbook.

- Homework: 1). Do you believe what is deposited into you emerges out of you? Why or why not? 2). Complete page 31 in the workbook (you will need access to the internet).

Week 7- What's Being Deposited (Students will begin to understand the dangers of unhealthy relationships).

- Class: Review chapter 4 definitions, discuss essays from previous week, read pages 38-41, and complete pages 33-35 in the workbook.

- Homework: Do you think the music industry has a great deal of influence on this generation? Why or why not?

Week 8-Dat Baby Don't Look like Me (Students will understand the stereotypes and misconceptions of dealing with unhealthy individuals).

- Class: 1). Review chapter 4 definitions, read pages 41-42 (Dat baby don't look like me), and complete page 36 in the workbook. 2). Discuss the correlation of music as it relates to relationships.

- Homework: 1). Discuss with your parent/guardian how music was when they grew up. What are the similarities and differences you found as it relates to music then and now? 2). Complete pages 37-38 with your parents.

Week 9-Unknown Name (Students will understand the significance of not connecting to the right people as it relates to healthy relationship building).

- Class: Review chapter 4 definitions, read pages 42-46 in the book, and discuss the 15 qualities that are found on page 44-45.

- Homework: If you could add any additional qualities to the list on pages 44-45 what would they be and why?

Week 10-Hop Over Syndrome (Students will understand the dynamics of why males in our society have historically been unable to maintain healthy relationships).

- Class: Discuss chapter five definitions in the workbook, read pages 47-48 in the book, and complete pages 45-46 in the workbook. Invite guest speaker to talk to the females for the first 30 minutes of class. Males will complete page 47 and have discussion with male group leader for the first 30 minutes of class. Bring both genders back together for last half of class to discuss what they learned.

- Homework: Write a reflective paragraph on today's class. What was the most/least interesting thing that happened today?

Week 11- Guns vs. Butter (Students will explore principles shared in a popular movie in 2002 called "Baby boy". Students will be able to identify the characteristics of guns and butter).

- Class: Review chapter 5 definitions, read pages 49-51 in the book, and complete pages 48-48 in the workbook.

- Homework: In the beginning scene of the movie "Baby Boy" Tyrese (Jodie) was trapped inside of his mother's womb as a grown man. In your own words explain what being trapped means to you?

Week 12-Guns vs. Butter (Cont'd)

- Class: Review chapter 5 definitions, read pages 52-53 in the book, complete page 50 in the workbook, and discuss highlights of "Baby boy" movie.

- Homework: 1).Watch the movie "Baby boy" (only with permission from your parents). 2).Write down 5 things you learned while watching the movie?

Week 13-Switching Process (Males will understand the role switching process and how this creates unlimited success).

- Class: 1). Review chapter 5 definitions, read pages 53-56 in the book and complete page 51 in the workbook. 2). Discuss the roles of males in the 21st century and the lack of leadership within our society.

- Homework: What male would you consider to be a true leader and why?

Week 14- Power of It's OK- (Males will understand the importance of applying the 30 It's OK principles).

- Class: Review chapter 5 definitions, read page 57 in the book, and complete pages 52-53 in the workbook.

- Homework: Name 10 additional tips you could add to the list of 25 from page 66?

Week 15- Three Questions (Students and adults will understand the importance of how these three questions will help them move forward in life).

- Joint Class: This class session is designed to close the communication gap between the parents and students. Have both the parents and students discuss chapter 6 definitions in the workbook, read pages 61-65 in the book, and complete pages 59-60 in the workbook.

- Homework: What did you learn from both groups coming together?

Week 16- Noise vs. Sound (Students and adults will understand the power of communication through the role reversal process).

- Joint Class: Review chapter 6 definitions, read pages 65-68 in the book, and complete pages 61-62 in the workbook.

- Homework: Do you think the social media (Facebook, Twitter, Skype, Oovoo, and etc...) has a major influence on this generation? Why or why not?

Week 17- We Don't Understand Each Other (Students will learn how to bridge the communication gap with their parents/guardians or educators).

- Joint Class: Review chapter 6 definitions, read pages 68-71 in the book, and complete pages 63-64 in the workbook.

- Homework: Read pages 71-75 in the book. Do you agree or disagree with the tips that educators should utilize on a daily basis?

Week 18- Prepared to Become Successful (Students will learn the five essential steps of preparation as it relates to being successful).

- Class: Discuss chapter seven definitions in the workbook, read pages 77-80 in the book, and complete pages 70-71 in the workbook.

- Homework: What are some other tips you can use which will help you be successful in life?

Week 19- Motivated to Become Successful (Students will learn the five essential steps of staying motivated during the discouraging times of life).

- Class: Review chapter 7 definitions, read pages 81-83 in the book, and complete page 72 in the workbook.

- Homework: Why is it so hard for people to stay motivated?

Week 20- Destined to Become Successful (Students will learn the five essential steps of being destined for greatness in life).

- Class: 1). Review chapter 7 definitions, read pages 83-85 in the book, and complete page 73 in the workbook. 2). Have the students to read the skit on pages 74-83.

- Homework: Complete pages 83, 85, and 93-94 and turn these in to your teacher/ facilitator next week.

R.E.N.E.W. Celebration

- Celebrate all the students who completed the R.E.N.E.W. curriculum

CHAPTER ONE

R.E.N.E.W. (Removing Every Negative Emotion & Word) Questionnaire

PLEASE DO NOT PUT YOUR NAME ON THIS FORM

Grade_____ Age_____ School_____ Sex M_____ F_____

My greatest struggle is (**a struggle is defined as something you want to change about yourself but just don't know how**)

_____

_____

_____

_____

_____

If there was one thing I could change about myself it would be the way I (**Ex: the way I think**)

_____

_____

_____

_____

_____

This is one question I would like to discuss during our weekly R.E.N.E.W. sessions (**Ex: Why won't you explain yourself?**)

_____

_____

_____

_____

_____

What is one question you have always wanted to ask an adult but never had the courage to (**Ex: Why are grownups so serious all the time?**)

_____

_____

_____

_____

_____

"History repeats itself because no one was listening the first time."
Anonymous

Chapter One Definitions

➢ **Idle:** (1) lacking worth or basis; vain (2) having no evident of lawful means or support; having no value, use or support (3) worthless; useless; pointless

➢ **Word:** (1) sound or combination of sounds; something said; utterance; remark or comment (2) discourse of talk or speech

➢ **Damage:** (1) occurrence of a change for the worse; injury or harm to a person or thing resulting in a loss in soundness and value

➢ **House:** (1) structure serving as a dwelling; natural covering that encloses or protects (2) place in which something is kept

❖ *Use page 9 in the workbook to jot down any thoughts you may have as you answer the questions in Chapter 1.*

Prior to reading Chapter One (optional), answer the following questions:

1. Did you ever hear the saying "what you don't know won't hurt you?" What does this saying mean to you?

   _____

   _____

   _____

   _____

   _____

2. Have you ever been told "what goes on in this house stays in this house" What comes to mind when you hear this saying?

   _____

   _____

   _____

   _____

   _____

3. What are some idle (worthless, useless, pointless) sayings you say to others on a regular basis (Ex: "you drove, "that's gay", "if you say so")? Before today did you know what the word idle meant?

   _____

   _____

   _____

   _____

   _____

4. Did you have difficulty answering any of the questions on the R.E.N.E.W questionnaire on pages 1&2? If so, which question was the most difficult to answer out of the four?

   _____

   _____

   _____

   _____

   _____

❖ *Before proceeding any further read pages 1- 6. Be sure to stop before reading the "Damaged House" section of the book (optional)*

Power of Idle Words

After reading the section "What you don't know won't hurt you" in the book answer the following questions (you can answer without reading the book).

1. Do you feel that things of the past have nothing to do with you? Explain.

   _____
   _____
   _____
   _____
   _____
   _____
   _____

2. What are some things that have hurt you that you were unaware of (Ex: lies, secrets, etc...)? How were you hurt (Ex: emotionally, physically, mentally, etc...)?

   _____
   _____
   _____
   _____
   _____
   _____
   _____

3. Words possess power. Do you think that some of your idle (worthless, useless, pointless) sayings have helped to create some of the circumstances and situations you now face? (Ex: you drove, "that's gay, "if you say so") Explain.

   _____
   _____
   _____
   _____
   _____
   _____

4. What damage do you think has been done to you over the years by the words (remarks, comments, or phrases) that have been said to you by others? Have those words become a part of your house (state of mind)?

_____

_____

_____

_____

_____

_____

_____

> *Have an open forum discussion on the power words possess. What is spoken, can and will manifest. Ponder the following quote "LIFE and DEATH lie within the power of the tongue."*

What are your thoughts about this quote, "Life and death are in the power of the tongue"? What does this mean to you? Do you believe that words have power? What is the most hurtful thing someone has ever said to you? Did you ever get over those words or did you start to believe what was said about you?

_____

_____

_____

_____

_____

_____

_____

_____

_____

_____

_____

_____

_____

❖ *Before proceeding any further read the remaining pages of this chapter (optional)*

Damaged House

➢ What you hear over and over becomes deeply embedded in your mind. Your "house" (state of mind) becomes cluttered, not only by what you hear, but also by the things you see and experience. Take a moment and just reflect over the past five years of your life. As you reflect are there any negative situations you would like to move forward from? What steps can you take to declutter (get rid of mess or disorder) from your house (state of mind)? List as many steps as you can think of.

_____
_____
_____
_____
_____

Now that you have completed reading Chapter one you can answer the questions at the end of the chapter (only if you have read the book). You may use this page to write your answers.

1. _____
_____
_____
_____
_____

2. _____
_____
_____
_____
_____

3. _____
_____
_____
_____
_____

Chapter One Reflections

"History repeats itself because no one was listening the first time."
Anonymous

<u>Thoughts to Remember</u>

❖ Speaking idle words will create destruction in our lives. What is spoken can impact us both negatively and positively. Your words form your world!

❖ It's time to clean your "house" (state of mind). What happens in your house no longer has to stay in your house. YOU CAN RELEASE IT!

<u>Question to Consider</u>

❖ What are you speaking over your life and the lives of others?

<u>Point to Ponder</u>

❖ What you don't know won't hurt you; it can KILL you!

<u>Quote to Carry</u>

❖ "Sometimes you have to remove yourself (get rid of distractions) so you can see yourself"- Marquis Cooper, Sr.

NOTES

CHAPTER TWO

"The past holds the key to the present, and the present holds access to the future"
Marquis Cooper, Sr.

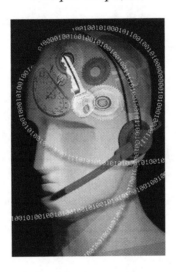

Who are these people and what role did they play in history
(read page 13 for more information on each of them)

> **Martin L. King, Jr.**   **Dr. C Everett Koop**   **Rosa Parks**
> **Gabriel Garcia Marquez**   **Christopher Columbus**   **Sacajawea**
> **William Lynch**

1. Have you heard of all the above people? Yes _____ No _____
   Which names haven't you heard before (just list their last names)?

   _____

2. Have you ever felt because you were not born when most of the above individuals were born
   that the past has nothing to do with you? Why?

   _____

   _____

   _____

Use page 18 in the workbook to jot down any thoughts you may have as you answer the questions in Chapter 2.

3. Have you ever heard the following statement, "What's done in the past should stay in the past?" Explain why you may feel this way about past events or people of the past.

_____

_____

_____

_____

_____

_____

_____

_____

_____

_____

4. Which person could you identify with the most and why? What was one similarity you noticed all the people in the past had (**please refer to page 13 for details on each person**)?

_____

_____

_____

_____

_____

_____

_____

_____

_____

_____

_____

What did they do???

- **Dr. Martin L. King, Jr.** minister, civil rights activist, winner of the Nobel Peace Prize and founder of the Southern Christian Leadership Conference. Dr. King led the Montgomery Bus Boycott and delivered the "I Have a Dream" speech in 1963. He used nonviolent methods to end racial segregation and racial discrimination.

- **Rosa Parks's** civil rights activist known as "the mother of the freedom movement". Rosa refused to obey bus driver, and give up her seat to make room for a white passenger which ignited the Montgomery Bus Boycott.

- **Christopher Columbus** was an explorer, colonizer, and navigator born in the Republic of Genoa, in what is today northwestern Italy.

- **Dr. C Everett Koop** U.S surgeon general who performed groundbreaking surgical procedures on conjoined twins & invented techniques commonly used today for infant surgery. Dr. Koop was the recipient of the Albert Schweitzer prize for humanitarians.

- **Gabriel Garcia Marquez** was a Columbian novelist, screenwriter, short story writer, & journalist. He won the Nobel Peace Prize in literature.

- **Sacajawea** accompanied Lewis & Clark during their Corps of discovery of the western U.S. in 1806.

- **William Lynch** purportedly delivered an address to an audience of slave owners on the banks of the James River in 1712 regarding control of slaves within the colony. The letter is controversial because many historians consider it to be a hoax.

- ❖ *As you read pages 11-15 (optional), be mindful that the past holds the key to the present, and the present holds access to the future. You may not have been born back then, but what happened back then is still affecting you NOW!*

Letter 1...Just 5 Words

Do you remember this letter during your childhood?
"Will you be my girlfriend?" or "Will you be my boyfriend?"
Circle Yes, No, or Maybe

1. Have you ever written one of these letters? How did you feel as you waited for the recipient of the letter to respond?

   _____

   _____

   _____

   _____

2. Did you ever receive this type of letter while growing up? Did you ever receive a letter and not reply? Why didn't you reply to the letter that was given to you?

   _____

   _____

   _____

   _____

❖ *In Chapter One, you learned what you don't know won't hurt you; it can KILL YOU! Continue reading Chapter Two (optional), and take a moment to open this next letter so that you can LIVE!*

Letter 2...Just 105 Words

William Lynch illustrates this principle in the book, *The Willie Lynch letter and the making of a Slave.* These words are written, *"Then take the female run a series of tests on her to see if she will submit to your desires willingly. Test her in every way because she is the most important factor for good economics. If she shows any sign of resistance in submitting completely to your will, do not hesitate to use the bull whip on her to extract the last bit of bitch out of her. Take care not to kill her, for in doing so, you spoil good economics. When in complete submission she will train her off springs in the early years to submit to labor when they become of age".*

> **William Lynch** slave owner; purportedly delivered a speech in 1712 on the banks of the James River in Virginia to other slave owners that provided principles to keep slaves under complete control; Lynch set a vicious cycle in motion that still affects us today.

What are your thoughts on the paragraph above? Had you ever seen or read this letter before? What part stood out to you the most as you read these words? Why do you believe this message was only given to women?

_____

_____

_____

_____

_____

_____

_____

_____

1. After reading the above letter do you still feel that what happens in the past should stay in the past?
   Yes _____ **No** _____

2. Has reading the letter changed your point of view about anything in life? If so, what are some of the things that changed?

   _____

   _____

   _____

   _____

3. You may not have been born back then, but the two principles from 1712 are still in effect. The two principles were "to sleep with" and "to make a profit off of." Do you think what happened in the past is still affecting women in the 21st century?

_____

_____

_____

_____

_____

_____

➤ **Now that you have completed reading Chapter Two; answer the questions at the end of the chapter (only if you have read the book). You may use this page to write your answers.**

1. _____

_____

_____

_____

_____

_____

_____

2. _____

_____

_____

_____

_____

_____

_____

3. _____

_____

_____

_____

_____

_____

_____

Chapter Two Reflections

"The past holds the key to the present, and the present holds access to the future."
Marquis Cooper, Sr.

<u>Thoughts to Remember</u>

❖ It's time NOW that you obtain the keys from the past which will open the doors of opportunity within your present, and provide you with access to your future.

❖ The William Lynch letter set a vicious cycle in motion, but you have the power to break the cycle.

<u>Question to Consider</u>

❖ Do you still think what's done in the past should stay in the past?

<u>Point to Ponder</u>

❖ You may not have been born during the era in which the Lynch letter was written; however the words that were shared still plague us today.

<u>Quote to Carry</u>

❖ *"When your PRESENT is not in order your FUTURE is in danger of being chaotic"- Marquis Cooper, Sr.*

NOTES

CHAPTER THREE

"The past holds the key to the present, and the present holds access to the future."
Marquis Cooper, Sr.

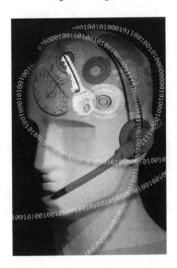

Chapter Three Definitions

➢ **Broken:** (1) thrown into a state of disarray or confusion (2) subdued or brought low in condition or status (3) weakened (4) out of working order

➢ **Family:** (1) any group of persons closely related by blood (2) basic social unit consisting of parents and their children

➢ **Dysfunctional:** (1) a breakdown of normal or beneficial relationships between members of a group (2) abnormal or impaired functioning

➢ **Fear:** (1) <u>F</u>alse <u>E</u>vidence <u>A</u>ppearing <u>R</u>eal (2) unpleasant feeling aroused by the threat of danger, evil, or pain

❖ *Use page 25 in the workbook to jot down any thoughts you may have as you answer the questions in Chapter 3.*

Prior to reading Chapter 3 (optional), take a moment to complete the table and answer the questions.

➤ **What does your family structure look like? Use the table below to show your family structure. Place an X in each box that represents those in your home.**

Father Stepfather	Mother Stepmother	Sister Stepsister	Brother Stepbrother	You	Other Grandparents, aunt, uncle, cousins, etc

1. Males: Are you the only or oldest male in your home? Are you seen as or thought of as the "man of the house"...if so how do you handle this role?

_____

_____

_____

_____

_____

_____

_____

_____

_____

_____

_____

2. Females: Are you in a family in which your father is not in the home? Has your mother taught you to be independent? What are your thoughts about being an independent woman?

_____

_____

_____

_____

_____

_____

_____

_____

_____

_____

_____

3. For those of you that have or grew up with both parents in the home, what is/was your family like? Who made the decisions in the home? Did your parents work together as one unit? If you didn't grow up with both parents in the home, what is/was your family like?

_____

_____

_____

_____

_____

_____

_____

_____

_____

_____

_____

_____

4. Do you think growing up in a "dysfunctional family" is worse than growing up in a "broken family"? Please use the definitions from page 19 to help make your case.

_____

_____

_____

_____

_____

_____

_____

_____

_____

_____

_____

_____

❖ In Chapter One you learned "what you don't know won't hurt you; it can KILL you." In Chapter Two you learned that even though you were not born back then, the past has a way of affecting the present. *Now I urge you to read pages 21-31 of Chapter 3 (optional), and open the letter to get a better understanding of how the past has helped shape many of our family structures.*

Letter 3...Just 110 Words

Lynch shares these words with the slave owners, *by her being left alone, unprotected, with the MALE IMAGE DESTROYED; the ordeal caused her to move from a psychological dependent state to a frozen independent state. In this frozen psychological state of independence she will raise her MALE and female offspring in reversed roles. For FEAR of the young males life she will psychologically train him to be MENTALLY WEAK and DEPENDENT but PHYSICALLY STRONG. Because she has become psychologically independent, she will train her female off spring to be psychologically independent. What have you got? You've got the nigger woman out front and the man behind and scared. This is a perfect situation for sound sleep and economic.*

Complete the table and have an open forum discussion over this table once you are finished.

> **In the table below, provide an example of what these words mean to you!!**

Part One	Part Two	Part Three
Then	**Then**	**Then**
By her being left alone, unprotected, with the male image destroyed, the ordeal caused her to move from a psychological dependent state to a frozen independent state.	*In this frozen psychological state of independence she will raise her male and female offspring in reversed roles.*	*For fear of the young male's life, she will psychologically train him to be MENTALLY WEAK and DEPENDENT but PHYSICALLY STRONG.*
Now	**Now**	**Now**

Now that you have completed reading Chapter Three, answer the questions at the end of the chapter (only if you read the book). You may use this page to write your answers.

1. _____
_____
_____
_____
_____
_____
_____
_____
_____
_____

2. _____
_____
_____
_____
_____
_____
_____
_____
_____
_____

3. _____
_____
_____
_____
_____
_____
_____
_____
_____

Chapter Three Reflections

"The past holds the key to the present, and the present holds access to the future."
Marquis Cooper, Sr.

<u>*Thoughts to Remember*</u>

❖ The principles shared in letter 2 and 3 created dysfunctional family structures. In order to begin to repair the damage which was caused, we must first understand that the dysfunctional or broken family structure is NOT simply the absence of a parent or parents, but it is the result of ROLE REVERSAL.

❖ Now is the time that we all begin to function in our rightful roles.

<u>*Question to Consider*</u>

❖ What is my rightful role as a man/woman?

<u>*Point to Ponder*</u>

❖ The natural order of the family was destroyed which tainted the male image, and altered the female mentality; causing her to raise her children in reversed roles. Because of this, we are currently faced with *"a nation of pant SAGGING, interchangeable grill mouth WEARING, bling bling WANTING, big rims SEEKING, foul language USING, sports driven DREAMERS, fashion statement MAKERS, non vision HAVING, no purpose in life WANTING, silly acting DAILY, non identity HAVING, name SEEKERS."*

NOTES

CHAPTER FOUR

"I was Responsible for waiting on you, I was Accountable in my search for you, I was Consistent in finding you, and now I have to be Persistent that I don't lose you"
Marquis Cooper, Sr.

Chapter Four Definitions

- ➤ **Deposit:** (1) to put in or set down (2) to lay down or leave behind by a natural process

- ➤ **Marriage:** (1) a legal or religious ceremony in which two people pledge themselves to each other in a manner of a husband and a wife (2) any close or intimate association or union (3) a blending or matching of different elements

- ➤ **Unknown:** (1) not within the range of one's knowledge, experience, or understanding (2) unidentified (3) unfamiliar

- ➤ **Bruh:** (1) used by African American males in everyday vocabulary to greet one another (2) Another way of saying bro (3) It is used as either a greeter or every day sentence hinter

- ➤ **Man:** (1) an adult male person as distinguished from a boy or woman (2) physiologically equipped to initiate conception but not to bear children (3) a husband

- ❖ *Use page 41 in the workbook to jot down any thoughts you may have as you answer the questions in Chapter 4.*

"I was Responsible for waiting on you, I was Accountable in my search for you, I was Consistent in finding you, and now I have to be Persistent that I don't lose you"
Marquis Cooper, Sr.

1. What does the above quote mean to you?

   _____

   _____

   _____

   _____

   _____

   _____

2. What qualities or characteristics are important to you when a male or female tries to talk to you? Why?

   _____

   _____

   _____

   _____

   _____

   _____

3. Have you ever heard the following statements "A good woman is hard to find" or "A piece of man is better than no man at all?" What are your thoughts about these statements?

   _____

   _____

   _____

   _____

   _____

4. How do the statements in question three influence the way you view males or females?

   _____

   _____

   _____

   _____

   _____

   _____

You can't say, "Sista let me tell you," until you first know what someone has told them...

➤ **FEMALES ONLY...answer the following 3 questions on a separate sheet of paper and give them to the group leader. DO NOT put your name on your answer sheet! The group leader will need to list all the answers on a board that can be viewed by all participants. When the list is ready, have an open forum discussion with the females regarding the answers listed. Have the females put a tally mark on a sheet of paper when they see an answer that affects them. After the discussion has ended, bring the males back in, but be sure to allow the males to view this list so that they are aware of the females' struggles. This is a great opportunity for the males to express their thoughts regarding the issues that young ladies are faced with.**

1. My greatest struggle is (a struggle is defined as something you want to change about yourself but don't know how to)

   _____

2. If there was one thing I could change about myself, it would be the way I

   _____

3. What is one question you have always wanted to ask an adult but never had the courage to?

   _____

❖ In Chapter One you learned "what you don't know won't hurt you; it can KILL you." In Chapter Two you learned that even though you were not born back then, the past has a way of affecting the present. In Chapter Three you received a better understanding of how the past has helped shape many of our family structures. *Now, begin reading "name search" and "purpose vs. appointment" in Chapter 4 (optional).*

Now that you have completed reading the "Name Search" (pg 34-36) and "Purpose vs. Appointment" (pg 36-38) sections, take a moment to answer and discuss the following questions (**you can still answer the questions without having the book**).

Name Search

1. What does your name mean? (Google your name using the internet search browser). If you can't find the meaning ask a family member to tell you why you were given your name?

    _____

    _____

    _____

    _____

2. Did you have difficulty finding the meaning of your name? If so, why do you think it was difficult?

    _____

    _____

    _____

    _____

3. If you were able to find the meaning of your name, are you inspired to become what your name says about you? Explain.

    _____

    _____

    _____

    _____

    _____

4. After completing the name search activity find one item which describes your name in the past and one item which describes your name now? What two items did you choose and why?

    _____

    _____

    _____

    _____

    _____

➤ Purpose vs. Appointment

A bruh has four purposes: 1) says what sounds good to get what they can 2). They're going to get what you got, 3) they're going to go tell about what they got and 4). They're going to destroy your name. On the other hand, a man has four appointments: 1) He's a king which means he cares deeply 2). He's a warrior which means he contends courageously 3). He's a mentor which means he communicates transparently and 4). He's a friend which means he connects deliberately.

1. Females: Now that you know the four purposes of a bruh, and the four appointments of men, which one do you run into the most? Why do you think this is the case?

    _____
    _____
    _____
    _____
    _____
    _____

2. Males: Which category do you think you currently fall under the "bruh" or "man"? Do you think males are taught more like the "bruh" or more like the "man"? Why?

    _____
    _____
    _____
    _____
    _____
    _____

3. Make a list of the men and bruh that you know or have encountered in the past. Which male from your list has the greatest influence on your life? What category is he under? How and why does this male influence you the most?

    _____
    _____
    _____
    _____
    _____
    _____
    _____

❖ *Prior to reading, "who are you married to", and "what's being deposited" (optional), review the information and answer the following question.*

Each Time you choose another partner, your chance of contracting a sexually transmitted disease goes up drastically. According to the Alan Guttmacher Institute "many teenagers, as well as adults, are indirectly exposed to more than one sexual partner each year because their partner has had sex with someone else" (1994). In addition, today's diversity is the new norm which has totally alienated the blue print, purpose, and the origin of the family (Jones, 1995). To make the situation more complex, family households containing children are now seeing a decline in the nuclear family structure and a rise in the extended family and single parent structure across the nation. To make matters worse, as the nation continues to see a decrease in the family structure, we also see a drastic decline in the level of engagement in children and their parents.

In 2009 the U.S. Census Bureau did a study on the number of single parents and the amount of child support they received (does not represent all single parents).[1] The bureau reported that there was an estimated 13.7 million single parents who had custody of 21.8 million children age 21 and under. Mothers accounted for 82.6% and fathers accounted for 17.4%. Yes, that is true. The results prove that we have more single women raising children alone. The numbers don't lie. This is primarily due to single mothers having to take on the responsibility of being both the mother and father in child rearing. As a result of a limited availability of any parental structure this has caused an epidemic which is seemingly growing out of control. Former U.S. Surgeon General C. Everett Koop, M.D., states "when you have sex with someone, you are having sex with everyone they have had sex with for the last ten years, and everyone they and their partners have had sex with for the last ten years". This led to the study and development of the sexual exposure chart which can be found by visiting the following website **http://www.chastity.com/node/227**.

> ➤ **"According to the paragraph (on page 33), when you have sex with someone, you are having sex with everyone they have had sex with for the last ten years, and everyone they and their partners have had sex with for the last ten years."** *(C. Everett Koop, M.D., Former U.S. Surgeon General)*

1. What are your thoughts regarding the information from above? Do you think the information is true? Do you feel like teenagers never think about things until something bad happens? What can you do in your school to bring awareness to this issue?

_____

_____

_____

_____

_____

_____

_____

_____

_____

_____

---

1   Grall, Timothy , US Census Bureau, *Custodial Mothers and Fathers and their Child Support: 2007.* (updated 2008 April ;sited 2012 May 31) available from: http://www.census.gov/prod/2009pubs/p60-237.pdf

_____

_____

_____

_____

_____

_____

_____

_____

_____

_____

_____

_____

_____

_____

_____

_____

_____

_____

_____

_____

_____

_____

_____

_____

_____

_____

_____

_____

_____

❖ *Continue reading pages 38-45 of Chapter 4 (optional) in order to gain more clarity on your true role and purpose in life.*

Will you marry me?

1. Did you have knowledge of the connection sex creates between people and their partners?
   Yes _____ No _____

2. According to the paragraph on page 33, did you know that each time you have sex with a person you were sleeping with their past partners as well? Do you think girls have sex because they are looking for acceptance from a male or because they are clueless of whom they really are?

   _____
   _____
   _____
   _____
   _____
   _____
   _____

➤ What Is Being Deposited

1. Have you ever heard the statement "what's in you will eventually come out of you"
   Yes _____ No _____

2. After reading this section, what are your thoughts regarding the above statement?

   _____
   _____
   _____
   _____
   _____
   _____

3. Refer back to the answers you provided on page 30. Do you think the answers you provided could help males appreciate and respect you more?

   _____
   _____
   _____
   _____
   _____
   _____

➢ Dat Baby Don't Look Like Me

1. When you hear songs that are demeaning to women, how do they make you feel? Do you find them cute, funny, entertaining, disrespectful, derogatory, or foolish? Explain

_____
_____
_____
_____
_____
_____

2. How does the media & music influence how you view yourself?

_____
_____
_____
_____
_____
_____

3. What are the top 10 Hip Hop songs this year? What influence do these artists have on your generation?

_____
_____
_____
_____
_____
_____

4. Males: What can you do to help females understand the value of their names, as well as the importance of keeping their names?

_____
_____
_____
_____
_____
_____
_____

Parents: How many of these songs do you really know? You can't ask for any help or search online for answers when completing this activity (be honest). Once you are finished you can compare your answers with those of your child.

Directions: Match the correct artist with the correct song.

1.	I just call her boo	a.	Plies
2.	Make me proud	b.	Travis Porter
3.	Goin Steady	c.	Yo Gotti
4.	Round of Applause	d.	Drake
5.	Swag On	e.	Wacka Floka
6.	Ayy Ladies	f.	Soulja Boy
7.	5 Star Chic	g.	Shawty Putt
8.	Becky	h.	Tity Boi
9.	Dat Baby Don't Look Like Me	i.	Rocko
10.	I don't love her	j.	Gucci Mane

Are you familiar with any of the songs and/or artists? If so which ones?

_____

_____

Do you think the media and music plays a huge role in the language barrier which exists within this generation? Why or why not?

_____

_____

_____

_____

_____

_____

Do you feel what our youth watch and hear has aided in the break in communication? Explain your answer.

_____

_____

_____

_____

_____

_____

Students complete the exercise listed below and then answer the questions that follow. Once you are finished compare your answers with your parents.

Directions: Match the correct artist with the correct song.

1.	I just call her boo	a.	Plies
2.	Make me proud	b.	Travis Porter
3.	Goin Steady	c.	Yo Gotti
4.	Round of Applause	d.	Drake
5.	Swag On	e.	Wacka Floka
6.	Ayy Ladies	f.	Soulja Boy
7.	5 Star Chic	g.	Shawty Putt
8.	Becky	h.	Tity Boi
9.	Dat Baby Don't Look Like Me	i.	Rocko
10.	I don't love her	j.	Gucci Mane

How do these artists and/or the lyrics to these songs influence the way you communicate with your parents?

_____

_____

_____

_____

_____

_____

_____

_____

_____

In chapter 1 you learned what you hear over and over becomes deeply embedded in your mind. Do you feel that the music you listen to has cluttered your "house" (state of mind) making it difficult to communicate and express yourself? Explain.

_____

_____

_____

_____

_____

_____

_____

_____

Now that you have completed reading Chapter Four, answer the questions at the end of the chapter (only if you have read the book). You may use this page to write your answers.

1. _____

2. _____

3. _____

Chapter Four Reflections

"I was Responsible for waiting on you, I was Accountable in my search for you, I was Consistent in finding you, and now I have to be Persistent that I don't lose you."
Marquis Cooper, Sr.

Thoughts to Remember

❖ The sexual exposure chart reveals that a 10 year connection between partners occurs when you have sex, but what you read in chapter 4 (optional) revealed that this connection is deeper. It is believed that soul ties are created when sexual intercourse occurs; thus linking you to a person for life. Sex is not just something you do! It is a meaningful experience that should only occur when you are able to handle ALL the responsibilities that may accompany it!!!

Question to Consider

❖ Your name is valuable. Do you recognize the importance of keeping a good name?

Point to Ponder

❖ A young man will respect you as much as you respect yourself. The more you fall in love with yourself the deeper you can appreciate him. My desire is that he will be strong enough to wait for you because your NAME is worth more than anything he could ever offer you! REAL TALK

NOTES

CHAPTER FIVE

"When the man is out of place, the woman becomes displaced, and the children become misplaced"
Marquis Cooper, Sr.

Chapter Five Definitions

➢ **Appointment:** (1) prearranged meeting (2) an arrangement to do something or meet someone at a particular time and place

➢ **Purpose:** (1) the reason for which something is done (2) a result or effect that is intended or desired; an intention (3) an aim or a goal (4) the point

➢ **Displaced:** (1) to remove from the usual or proper place (2) to place in another situation (3) to take the place of

➢ **Misplaced:** (1) to put into a wrong place or position (2) having the arrangement disturbed

❖ *Use page 55 in the workbook to jot down any thoughts you may have as you answer the questions in Chapter 5.*

"When the man is out of place, the woman becomes displaced, and the children become misplaced"

1. What are your thoughts regarding the above statement? Do you see this family structure on a daily basis? What can we do to change this?

    _____
    _____
    _____
    _____
    _____
    _____
    _____

2. Do you think more "males" or "females" are displaced (refer to the definition on page 44) in our society? What can we do to fix this problem?

    _____
    _____
    _____
    _____
    _____
    _____
    _____

3. Read the following and give your thoughts on how we begin to change this: _a nation of pant SAGGING, interchangeable grill mouth WEARING, bling bling WANTING, big rims SEEKING, foul language USING, sports driven DREAMERS, fashion statement MAKERS, non vision HAVING, no purpose in life WANTING, silly acting DAILY, non identity HAVING, name SEEKERS... Can we do anything to change this image in America?_

    _____
    _____
    _____
    _____
    _____
    _____
    _____
    _____
    _____

The guns and butter concept was discussed in a popular 2002 movie called Baby Boy which starred singer and song writer Tyrese (Jodie). In the movie, Ving Rhames (Melvin) stated there were two types of guys; ones that had guns and ones that had butter. Guns were described as making investments and getting and maintaining a healthy lifestyle. Butter, on the other hand was acquiring material things like cars, clothes, and homes. He used the concept of guns and butter to contrast the two walks of life.

4. **What are three to four things that come to mind when you hear the following terms:**

(a) Guns

_____

_____

_____

(b) Butter

_____

_____

_____

(c) King

_____

_____

_____

(d) Warrior

_____

_____

_____

(e) Mentor

_____

_____

_____

(f) Friend

_____

_____

_____

You can't say, "Bruh if you only knew," until you first hear what the bruhs have to say...

> **MALES ONLY**...answer the following 3 questions on a separate sheet of paper and give them to the group leader. **DON'T put your name on your answer sheet!** The group leader will need to list all the answers on a board that can be viewed by all participants. When the list is ready, have an open forum discussion with the males regarding the answers listed. Have males put a tally mark on a sheet of paper when they see an answer that affects them. After the discussion has ended, bring the females back in the room and allow them to view the list. This is a great opportunity for females to express their thoughts regarding the issues that males are faced with on a daily basis

1. My greatest struggle is (a struggle is defined as something you want to change about yourself but don't know how)

   _____

   _____

   _____

2. If there was one thing I could change about myself, it would be the way I

   _____

   _____

   _____

5. What is one question you have always wanted to ask an adult but never had the courage to?

   _____

   _____

   _____

❖ In Chapter One you learned "what you don't know won't hurt you; it can KILL you." In Chapter Two you learned that even though you were not born back then, the past has a way of affecting the present. In Chapter Three you received a better understanding of how the past has helped shape many of our family structures. Chapter 4 revealed the whispers of "Sista let me tell ya!" ***Now, READ CHAPTER 5 (optional) because it's time to speak to the males because "Bruh if you only knew" what would you do?***

➢ **<u>Hop Over Syndrome</u>**

1. In your own words describe the "hop over" syndrome?

   _____

   _____

   _____

   _____

   _____

   _____

2. Females: Why do think males have problems being in committed relationships as they get older?

   _____

   _____

   _____

   _____

   _____

   _____

3. Do you find it difficult to talk to one person for a long period of time? In your eyes why do you think this is so hard to do?

   _____

   _____

   _____

   _____

   _____

   _____

4. Do you feel this generation of males has lost their potential to be successful in life? If so, why do you think it's affecting more males than females?

   _____

   _____

   _____

   _____

   _____

   _____

   _____

➤ What to Look For

1. Males: Do you think having a healthy relationship with your mother is important? Do you think the way you treat or talk to your mother will carry over into future relationships? Why or why not?

   _____

   _____

   _____

   _____

   _____

   _____

2. What does this quote mean to you, "You come to love not by finding the perfect person, but by finding an imperfect person perfectly"- Sam Keen

   _____

   _____

   _____

   _____

   _____

   _____

3. Do you think it's important to be genuinely concerned with trying to get to know a young lady or young man for who they are? Why or why not?

   _____

   _____

   _____

   _____

   _____

   _____

4. Females: Why do you think we have a society of males that neglect, ignore, demean, disrespect, criticize, and make females feel invaluable?

   _____

   _____

   _____

   _____

   _____

   _____

➤ **Guns vs. Butter**

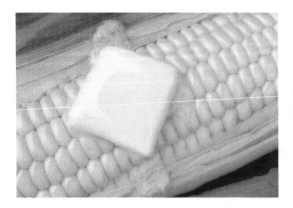 

1. As you analyze these two pictures what words immediately come to your mind?

   _____

   _____

   _____

   _____

2. Males are often taught to be hard in life and not show any type of emotions. Do you think this is healthy? Why? Why not?

   _____

   _____

   _____

   _____

3. What advice would you give to a male who came to you and said "how can I get respect without being a thug"?

   _____

   _____

   _____

   _____

4. Males often feel like the world has given up on them. Do you think there is any truth to this statement? If so what can we do to change this process in America?

   _____

   _____

   _____

   _____

➢ <u>Switching Process</u>

1. Why do you think society views men as unsympathetic, uncaring, and unaffectionate?

_____

_____

_____

_____

_____

_____

2. How do you see this quote now compared to when you first saw it in chapter four, *"I was Responsible for waiting on you, I was Accountable in my search for you, I was Consistent in finding you, and now I have to be Persistent that I don't lose you"*?

_____

_____

_____

_____

_____

_____

3. Females: The "hop over" syndrome is when males ignore anything or anyone that's beneficial to them. What can you do to help change this type of mindset?

_____

_____

_____

_____

_____

_____

4. Males: What will you do now to begin living up to the meaning of your name and resume your rightful role by becoming the king, warrior, mentor, and friend a man is intended to be?

_____

_____

_____

_____

_____

_____

➢ Power of It's OK

Males: Look at the following 25 It's OK traits. If you agree with the trait place a Y in the box. If you disagree with the trait place an N in the box. Once you are finished count up your Y's and N's and list them on the lines below.

1. "It's Ok" to be intelligent _____
2. "It's OK," to break and lead at the same time _____
3. "It's OK," not to use slang _____
4. "It's OK" to speak correct English _____
5. "It's OK," if you don't want to play sports _____
6. "It's OK," not to sag _____
7. "It's OK," if you don't want a grill in your mouth _____
8. "It's OK," not to have rims on your car _____
9. "It's OK," not to act silly _____
10. "It's OK," to open the car door for a lady when you go out on a date_____
11. "It's OK" to be respectful to all adults _____
12. "It's OK," to shake a young ladies hand and say goodnight _____
13. "It's OK," to kiss her on the cheek after a date _____
14. "It's OK," to use your manners _____
15. "It's OK," to clean your room _____
16. "It's OK," to vacuum the house _____
17. "It's OK," to clean the bathroom _____
18. "It's OK," to run your mom some bath water _____
19. "It's OK," to rub your mom's feet _____
20. "It's OK" to be a leader and not a follower _____
21. "It's OK" not to use profanity _____
22. "It's OK" to have a vision _____
23. "It's OK" to know your purpose in life _____
24. "It's OK" to be butter (cover and protect) _____
25. "It's OK" to be you _____

Number of Y's _____
Number of N's _____

Did you have more Y's or N's? Which three things are the most difficult for most males to do? Why?

_____

_____

_____

_____

_____

_____

_____

After completing the questions in Chapter 5 how would you describe the following terms now?

(a) Guns

_____

_____

_____

_____

(b) Butter

_____

_____

_____

_____

(c) King

_____

_____

_____

_____

(d) Warrior

_____

_____

_____

_____

(e) Mentor

_____

_____

_____

_____

(f) Friend

_____

_____

_____

_____

Chapter Five Reflections

"When the man is out of place, the woman becomes displaced, and the children become misplaced"
Marquis Cooper, Sr.

<u>*Thoughts to Remember*</u>

❖ The circle of change begins with knowing the power of "It's OK"

❖ Every time you switch roles, you become somebody else to someone else; but you **HAVE** to remain the same in who you are!

❖ Butter **PROTECTS**; it **DOES NOT** damage!

<u>*Question to Consider*</u>

❖ A man's strength is in his character. Does your character reflect four purposes or four appointments?

<u>*Point to Ponder*</u>

❖ It's not an easy task taking something hard and cold (***Gun***), and shaping it into something soft enough to take on whatever form is needed at any given moment (***Butter***). However, the *Gun* mentality must become *Butter* mentality. In order to change the male mentality; the female mentality must be willing to release the tight grip she has on the *Gun*! Women, it's time we allow men to become *Butter* so that they can cover us, protect us, and keep us from sticking to the wrong stuff!

NOTES

CHAPTER SIX

"If you listen to the whispers, you won't have to hear the screams"
Cherokee Proverb

Chapter Six Definitions

➤ **Sound:** (1) free from error (2) whole, stable, healthy, rational, or valid

➤ **Noise:** (1) loud, confused, senseless or shouting (2) unwanting (3)undesired (4) unpleasant

➤ **Language:** (1) a body of words and the systems for their use common to a people who are of the same community or nation (2) communication by voice in a distinctly human manner (3) systems of linguistic signs or symbols considered in the abstract (opposed to speech)

➤ **Barrier:** (1) any natural bar or obstacle (2) anything that restrains or obstructs progress, access, etc…

➤ **Communication:** (1) the act of process of communicating (2)the imparting or exchange of thoughts, opinions, or information by speech, writing, or signs (3) something imparted, interchanged, or transmitted

❖ *In Chapter One you learned "what you don't know won't hurt you; it can KILL you." In Chapter Two you learned that even though you were not born back then, the past has a way of affecting the present. In Chapter Three you received a better understanding of how the past has helped shape many of our family structures. Chapter Four revealed the whispers of "Sista let me tell ya!" Chapter Five instructed males on becoming "Butter" for life.* **Now, it's time to have a bit of REAL TALK with parents and educators (youth you are welcome to stay in the room).**

➤ **PRIOR TO READING** (optional): **Parents and students please answer the following questions on a sheet of paper** (a) *My greatest struggle is* (b) *If there was one thing I could change about myself, it would be the way I* (c) *what is one question you always wanted to ask an adult while growing up but never had the courage to do...* **DON'T put your name on your paper! The group leader will need to list all the answers on a board that can be viewed by all participants. When the list is ready, have an open forum discussion with the parents and youth regarding the answers listed. Have the parents and youth put a tally mark on a sheet of paper when they see an answer that affects them.**

➤ ## PARENTS

1. How many answers do you have in common with your children? What did you learn from doing this simple activity?

   _____

   _____

   _____

   _____

   _____

   _____

   _____

   _____

2. Many of the answers may be similar among the parents and students. With this in mind, why do you think communication between youth and parents is so difficult?

   _____

   _____

   _____

   _____

   _____

   _____

   _____

   _____

   _____

   _____

   _____

   _____

YOUTH & YOUNG ADULTS

1. How many answers do you have in common with your parents? What did you learn from doing this activity?

_____

_____

_____

_____

_____

_____

2. Many of the answers may be similar to those of your parents. With this in mind, why do you feel as if adults don't hear and/or understand you?

_____

_____

_____

_____

_____

_____

_____

_____

_____

_____

_____

ALL

What can be done to tear down the barriers blocking effective communication between youth and adults?

_____

_____

_____

_____

_____

_____

_____

_____

_____

Activity: Give each parent and youth a copy of this chart. Have them to role play by reading the information in the opposite category. After you finish the activity answer the questions that follow. It's time to dialogue!!

10 Questions from TEENAGERS to PARENTS	10 Responses from PARENTS to TEENAGERS
1. Parents don't understand me and they never will.	1. You don't understand me either and you never will until you have children.
2. You don't trust me to do right once I mess up.	2. I trust you but sometimes you have to earn it back.
3. You won't let things go and continue to harp on them.	3. You won't let things go and remind me often of what I promised to do.
4. You bring up the past all the time.	4. You bring up the past and try to hurt me on certain things.
5. You won't allow me to make mistakes.	5. Learn from your mistakes without making the same ones over.
6. You can't communicate with me about my problems.	6. You can't communicate with me about my problems.
7. You are hard on me for every little thing I do.	7. You are hard on me for not being able to provide certain things at certain times.
8. You're not fair all the time.	8. You're not fair all the time.
9. You treat my siblings better than me	9. When you were younger I treated you the same way.
10. You throw things in my face especially when I do something you told me not to do.	10. You throw things in my face especially when I promise you something and now I can't make good on it.

How many similarities did you have in common? Which category caused the most dialogue between you and your child? Did you feel awkward at anytime during the role playing? Do you think this activity was helpful?

_____

_____

_____

_____

_____

All: Why do you feel that youth and adults just can't seem to relate to one another?

_____
_____
_____
_____
_____
_____
_____
_____

Youth: Oftentimes you feel as if no one is listening or even cares to listen. Has doing this exercise changed any of that? If so, how has it changed?

_____
_____
_____
_____
_____
_____
_____
_____
_____

Adults: Oftentimes you feel as if what you're saying is going in one ear and out the other when talking to youth. Has doing this exercise changed that? If so, how has it changed?

_____
_____
_____
_____
_____
_____
_____
_____

❖ *As an educator you play a vital role in the lives of youth. Almost 50% of children's time is spent with you. If you are interested in finding ways on how you can assist in bridging the communication gap, then read pages 71-75 (optional).*

Take a moment to have an open forum discussion regarding the information shared in the "Tips for Educators" section (optional).

Educators: Think back to the days in which you first decided to pursue a career as an educator. Is this still your reason for remaining an educator? What has changed?

_____

_____

_____

_____

_____

_____

Parents: Do you feel educators have lost the zeal for their jobs? Why do you feel educators are not as compassionate or dedicated as they were when you were in school?

_____

_____

_____

_____

_____

_____

Youth: Do you have a favorite teacher, counselor, principal, or any member of the school staff? Why is this person your favorite? What does he/she do that the other educators don't do?

_____

_____

_____

_____

_____

Educators: What kept your fire ignited so you never lost passion for what you are doing? Does that same passion still drive you today? Does it show when you are working with students and parents?

_____

_____

_____

_____

_____

Parents: What can you do to keep our educators motivated? Keep in mind YOUR children are in their hands, and our children are influenced both negatively and positively by ALL they encounter. How can you be more supportive of educators?

_____

_____

_____

_____

_____

Youth: I know it is the norm for adults to motivate and encourage you, but you can also return that same encouragement. How can you help educators better educate you?

_____

_____

_____

_____

_____

Educators: How can you use these tips to not just become a better educator, but to also aid in bridging the communication gap?

_____

_____

_____

_____

_____

ALL: Do you feel that using the tips and applying all that you have learned from the book thus far will increase parental involvement, student participation, and close the gap on students "celebrated" compared to those being "tolerated"? Explain.

_____

_____

_____

_____

_____

_____

Now that you have completed reading Chapter Six, answer the questions at the end of the chapter (only if you have the book). You may use this page to write your answers.

1. _____
   _____
   _____
   _____
   _____
   _____
   _____
   _____
   _____
   _____

2. _____
   _____
   _____
   _____
   _____
   _____
   _____
   _____
   _____
   _____
   _____
   _____

3. _____
   _____
   _____
   _____
   _____
   _____
   _____
   _____
   _____
   _____

Chapter Six Reflections

"If you listen to the whispers, you won't have to hear the screams"
Cherokee Proverb

Thoughts to Remember

❖ **Youth:** It's time to realize that adults understand you more than you give them credit for... just take the time and dialogue.

❖ **Adults:** The ONLY way to save some of our youth is to learn the language they speak!

Question to Consider

❖ **Youth:** Have your whispers become screams?

❖ **Adults**: Why must our children scream before we start listening?

Point to Ponder

❖ Our similarities far outweigh our differences. Our languages are not as complex as we make them. Sometimes the language we as parents and educators need to hear most is the unspoken language. The whispers are often what our youth keep in their 'houses" (state of mind. The unspoken (the screams) are the cries of the whispers we failed to hear. We can no longer allow the gap to stay open. NOW is the time to bridge ALL communication gaps and do whatever is necessary to save our youth.

NOTES

CHAPTER SEVEN

"If you leave and grow, you can come back and plant"
Marquis Cooper, Sr.

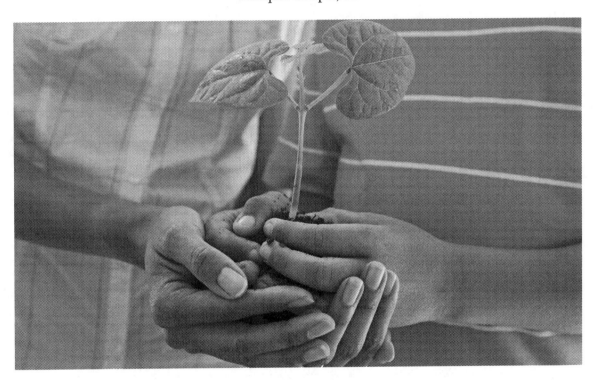

Chapter Seven Definitions

➤ **Prepared:** (1) to make or get ready beforehand for a specific purpose

➤ **Motivated:** (1) move to action (2) to give an incentive for action

➤ **Destined:** (1) to determine beforehand; preordained (2) to assign for a specific end, use, or purpose (3) meant to be; certain to occur

➤ **Success:** (1) good fortune (2) favorable outcome

"If you leave and grow, you can come back and plant"
-Marquis Cooper

1. What comes to mind when you read the above quote?

   _____

   _____

   _____

   _____

   _____

   _____

   _____

2. Who or what do you turn to for encouragement and motivation? Why?

   _____

   _____

   _____

   _____

   _____

   _____

   _____

   _____

3. Are you a leader or a follower? Explain.

   _____

   _____

   _____

   _____

   _____

   _____

   _____

   _____

In Chapter One you learned "what you don't know won't hurt you; it can KILL you." In Chapter Two you learned that even though you were not born back then, the past has a way of affecting the present. In Chapter Three you received a better understanding of how the past has helped shape many of our family structures. Chapter Four revealed the whispers of "Sista let me tell ya!" Chapter Five instructed males on becoming "Butter" for life. Chapter Six provided a bit of REAL TALK for parents, educators, and youth. **Now read the pages of 77-80 to find out what preparing for success is all about (optional).**

PREPARED TO BECOME SUCCESSFUL

1. Which one of the five areas of becoming successful do you struggle with the most (becoming complacent, people dictating your future, looking for handouts, becoming more assertive, or studying and applying yourself more)? Which one do you struggle with the least? Explain both answers

   _____
   _____
   _____
   _____
   _____
   _____

2. What does the following quote mean to you "when your vision is clear you never have to get dirty"?

   _____
   _____
   _____
   _____
   _____

3. Are there people in your life who validate (applaud) you for the positive things that you are doing? If so, what do you admire most about those individual (s)?

   _____
   _____
   _____
   _____
   _____

4. What are your goals in life and how do you plan on accomplishing those?

   _____
   _____
   _____
   _____
   _____

❖ *Are you ready to learn how to be motivated in life?" Read pages 81 to the bottom of page 83 to find out how (optional)*

MOTIVATED TO BECOME SUCCESSFUL

1. Which one of the five areas of motivation do you struggle with the most (not being motivated, waking up motivated, self encouragement, facing new challenges, or trying to help other people that don't want to be helped)? Which one do you struggle with the least? Explain both answers

_____

_____

_____

_____

_____

2. What motivates you to keep going in life? Are there times you feel like quitting or giving up in life? If so what happens when you feel this way?

_____

_____

_____

_____

_____

3. W.E.B. Dubois coined the Talented Tenth concept. This means the 10% that make it in life should bring the other 90% with them. Do you think this concept is being carried out in the 21st century?

_____

_____

_____

_____

_____

4. Teenagers often use slang terminology such as "you drove" to make their peers feel stupid as it relates to certain situations. After reading this section is there something or someone that's "driving you" not to stay motivated?

_____

_____

_____

_____

❖ *Are you ready to learn that you are destined to be successful?" Read the remaining pages of this chapter (optional)*

DESTINED TO BECOME SUCCESSFUL

1. Which one of the five areas of being destined for success do you struggle with the most (realizing you are in a battle, shutting the door on distractions, reconditioning your mind, resubmitting to original thoughts, or recommitting to yourself)? Which one do you struggle with the least? Explain both answers

   _____
   _____
   _____
   _____
   _____
   _____

2. What was something you received in school that meant the world to you? Do you still have it and if so why?

   _____
   _____
   _____
   _____
   _____
   _____

3. What does this quote mean to you, "If you can learn how not to be distracted while in the midst (middle) of distractions, you will be great in life"?

   _____
   _____
   _____
   _____
   _____
   _____

4. Which principle out of the 15 will benefit you the most as you move forward in life?

   _____
   _____
   _____
   _____
   _____
   _____

Group Activity

The following skit is designed to enhance and/or bring to life all of the situations that you have experienced within this curriculum. The skit sheds light on situations that our youth experience each day in this country. The skit is designed to bring awareness to the following; 1) eliminate idle sayings, 2) understand who you are so you won't become who you're not, 3) break away from unhealthy relationships, 4) teach you how to deal with unhealthy individuals, 5) help you make better decisions, 6) reduce teenage pregnancy, 7) bring awareness to teenage suicide, 8) help you be content with who you are, 9) understand the hidden message in music, and 10) close the communication gap between youth, parents, and educators.

The skit was written by two college students from Arkansas. The message behind the skit is to bring awareness to the many issues that are staring our youth in the face on a daily basis. The skit can be read together as a group, various students can be assigned roles, or the skit may be used as a mini drama production at your respective high school.

This skit was first performed in March 2010 by a group of seniors at Lee High School in Marianna, Arkansas. Once the students have finished the skit it would be a great idea to have an open forum discussion to deal with issues that may have been hidden. At the end of the activity there are questions designed to ignite further discussion, or the questions may be used as a self-reflective piece to see how the students processed the skit. In the words of the Cherokee Proverb, "If you listen to the whispers, you won't have to hear the screams." Sit back and enjoy "Sista let me tell ya, Bruh if you only knew."

"Sista Let Me Tell Ya, Bruh If You Only Knew"…
Written by: Mehla Duffy and Ashley Murphy

Characters:

- ❖ Narrator
- ❖ William Lynch (slave owner from 1712)
- ❖ Cindy (high school student)
- ❖ QT (star athlete and Marlon's brother)
- ❖ Marlon (bruh)
- ❖ Christopher (4.0 student)
- ❖ Girl (displaced mom)
- ❖ Son (misplaced child)
- ❖ Mom (single parent mother)
- ❖ Kesha (Marlon's girlfriend)
- ❖ Author (youth playing an adult)
- ❖ Child (slave girl)
- ❖ Jessica (Cindy's friend)

Narrator- We have often heard the words, "What happens in the past should stay in the past." Well, let's take a look at something that happened in 1712 that's still affecting us in 2012. Let's listen in on William Lynch's secret to the making of a slave……

William Lynch and slave girl- (walks in with authority and begins to talk to the audience)- Take the female, run a series of tests on her to see if she will submit to your desires willingly. Test her in every way because she is the most important factor for good economics. If she shows any sign of resistance in submitting completely to your will, do not hesitate to use the bull whip on her to extract the last bit of bitch out of her. (Pulls out a whip and acts as if to hit the female slave while still talking.) Take care not to kill her, (stops beating the slave at this point) for in doing so, you spoil good economics. When in complete submission she will train her offspring in early years to submit to labor when they become of age.

Scene 1:

Narrator- Let's just see how the William Lynch letter has affected us today. A young girl sits on the floor crying and talking to her son…..

Girl: I'm sorry you may never know your father. We don't need him anyway. I love you, son, and I'll be the best mother and father I can be. I guess you'll be the man of the house from now on.

Son: Mom, where's my father and why doesn't he ever come around?

Girl: It's a long story, son, and I really don't want to talk about it.

Son: But, mom, I really want to know what happened

Girl: OK! When I was younger I was with a lot of guys. Some treated me like dirt and some treated me like a beautiful queen, but I always fell for the ones who treated me like trash instead of the nice ones. I've done so many bad things in my past that I regret, but the one thing I don't regret is having you. I love you, son with all my heart and I promise to do any and everything I can to help you later in life. I don't want you to be anything like those guys I had to deal with or even like your father, whoever he may be. I'm going to teach you how to treat ladies like queens.

Son: It's okay, mama! I love you, too, and I don't wanna see you being treated like trash. I'm going to treat you and all the other women I meet just like princesses. God knows I don't want to be anything like those guys you described. I wanna be so much better than that and I promise I will.

Girl: Awwwww, son you're thinking like a man already and that's what I want.

Son: Let's not worry about my father. Although, I would love to know him, I'll be just fine with a loving, caring mother like you. You know not all mothers and sons have a good relationship like us, and that's what I'm thankful for (smiling and hugging his mother).

Scene 2:

Narrator-Cindy and Jessica are having a conversation about college. One of the girls wants to make money but not in the sense of going to school.

Cindy: (Looking frustrated while looking at college apps) Hmmm..... College Applications..... (Reads aloud) Write a 1,000-word essay about your biggest accomplishment...... (gets frustrated and rips the application) ...... (yells) I can't do this, college isn't for me! I'll just be a back-up dancer in the music videos...like the ones on BET so everybody can see me. I know I look good so I know all the rappers will want me to be a back-up dancer in their video.

Jessica: Girl, please! Don't nobody want you in their video.

Cindy: You just mad because you don't look as good as me.

Jessica: O, wow! Really, Cindy, really?

Cindy: Uh, Yeah, You Know you wish you had these curves and can twerk it like this (moves her body, dancing) whaaaaaaaat....what...what...what ...

Jessica: I wouldn't want to be in a video anyways. I'm focusing on going to college, getting a degree so I can do some things in life, know what I'm saying? O, right, that's right, you wouldn't know anything about college .You only know about BET videos and crap like that.

Cindy: Such a hater! Not only can I dance, I can also pull any guy I want at the snap of my fingers. I'm not into all that college stuff, now, that's what you call crap. You really need to take a chill pill and get like me, you heard me..

Jessica: You are something else, girl. I have some studying to do, unlike some people I know.

Cindy: Some people like who? I know you not talking about me because I have studying to do to as well. Right now I'm studying on how to pull that guy right there (points at a group of guys) ooooowwwe, he's a cutie.

Narrator- William Lynch wanted to instill two principles in black women but the problem is now affecting all women. Those two principles were she is only good enough "to sleep with" and the only thing she is suitable for is to "make a profit off."

Scene 3:

Narrator- The next day at school, during lunch, Marlon runs into Kesha. Kesha was talking with the girls and Marlon approaches her. QT was sitting nearby and overhears the entire conversation.

Marlon: I hit it, split it, and now I'm done with it!

Kesha: What?? What are you saying???

Marlon: Let me see the best way to explain this; I'm the teacher, you're the student, class was in session but now you've been dismissed. Deuces!!

Kesha: Please don't leave me, Marlon, I love you baby (**running after him**)

Kesha: I'll do anything you want baby.

Marlon: I'm so done, sweetie (**walks away shaking his head**)

(Kesha: sits in the corner trying to figure out what to do. The girls console her and they walk off the stage)

QT: Bro, that was cold....you sure you want to do that?

Marlon: Dude, I ain't trying to be no Daddy. What I look like? I just wanted to hit it and quit it. I did so and now I'm straight.

QT: O, dude that's so not right! But how was it? (laughing very hard)

Marlon: Awww, man get out of here with that! But it was nice, just what I wanted. I wasn't looking for anything serious. I just wanted some; you know what I'm saying?

Qt: Ummmmmm, so you saying you don't really like the girls you talk to?

Marlon: That's what I'm saying, man ..

QT: Basically, you just wanna hit it and be through with them!!

Marlon: Exactly, buddy, now you're thinking.

QT: Dude, that's like the weirdest thing ever. Aren't you afraid of catching something?

Marlon: Ay, chill out, dude. I know how to wrap it up. You sounding like somebody daddy-all serious and stuff. I don't wanna hear that stuff, I know what I'm doing, you just need to get with the show …

(QT just shakes his head and walks over to Cindy)

QT: Hey, girl, what's up? Why you got all these papers out at lunch….Ain't you tired of school work?

Cindy: Yes, I could be watching videos but Ms. Bee, the counselor, wants me to think about college and fill out the applications. She said I shouldn't miss the deadline to apply if I want to go.

QT: Why do you need to go to college? You know I'll go pro once I get discovered… You know I'll take care of you, girl….You know you my girl and you know I can hoop….And you know the way you backed that thing up on me last night…you don't have to worry about NO-THING!

Cindy: (LOL) Shut-up, QT…but um…Yeah… I was even thinking I could be a back-up dancer in the music videos. Hahahaha, you know me I can dance like whaaaaat…what…what, lol…..

Christopher: (walks over)- Hey, Ms. Bee told me to talk to you about college and see if you needed any help filling out college applications.

QT: Why do you even talk to this nerd? What kinda name is Christopher Columbus anyway? Was yo moma reading history books when she had you?

Christopher: And what kind of name is QT? What does it stand for….Q-tip?

QT: No, the Q stands for cool, get out of here.

Christopher: Cool starts with a C… Cindy, you know where to find me…. (walks away shaking his head)

Cindy: You didn't have to do Christopher like that. He's a nice person.

QT: What… you like that nerd? Gesh! What has Ms. Bee been putting in your head? ………

Cindy: He's a nice guy....Why you gotta be like that?

QT: What... you think he's better than me cuz he can spell a few words?! I don't need this, I hoop! (Yelling) I don't need you, that nerd, college or Ms. Bee so you can miss me with all of that mess!....

Cindy: But....

QT: (cuts her off) Save it!

Cindy: Lord, I don't know what I'm gone do with QT.

Scene 4

Narrator- Cindy and Christopher run into each other after school.

Christopher: Hey, can I talk to you for a second?

Cindy: Sure, What's up?

Christopher: I was just wondering if you would come with me to a book signing that my mentor is having.....you know, if you aren't doing anything tomorrow.

Cindy: Ummmmmm, OK, I'll think about it.

Christopher: Well, it will be tomorrow at 5:00 in our gym, so you won't have to worry about getting lost.

Cindy: Well gessssh 5:00 is kinda pushing it; I mean that's when I watch all the videos on BET..

Christopher: What's a BET ?

Cindy: O, wow, really? You gotta be kidding me...

Christopher: Ummmmm, No I'm not ..

Cindy: O, my kinda weird aren't we. Ummmm, let's see how can I explain this (thinking). Well.... its kinda sorta like, well, its like a video, ummmm, I can't really explain it. Let me just give you a demonstration. It's a music video and a rapper be rapping or whatever and there are girls in the background dancing like this (starts dancing)

Christopher: OOOOOooooooo OK, OK, OK, OK, I think I get the picture, but why are those videos so important to you?

Christopher: Aren't there other talents you have?

Cindy: Well, those backup dancers excite me and that's what I wanna do with my life. I'm not really interested in this whole college thing. I wanna be seen, I want to show my talent.

Christopher: Aren't there other talents you have?

Cindy: Of course there are silly, but none of them capture me like dancing in a video.

Christopher: Ooooooooooook, but like I was saying, I really hope you can make it to the book signing.

Cindy: Ok, I'll try!

Christopher: Ok, please try hard. It will really make me happy if you come.

Cindy: hehehehehehe, ooooook I have to go home … See ya later!!

Christopher: See Ya…

Scene 5

Narrator- Later, QT goes home and tries to talk to his mom about some of his frustrations.

QT: Hey, Ma, can I talk to you for a sec?

Mom: What is it, son? I'm tired. I had a bad day at work (**says as if not to really care, while laying her head on the table**).

QT: Why daddy don't ever come around?

Mom: Uh, don't ask me questions like that. I don't know, baby. Why you wanna bring up stuff like that and hurt moma? Do we have to talk about this? I've already explained that you may never know who he is.

QT: Moma, it's always about you! What about my scars. I'm scared I won't be nothing in life and end up just like my dad!

Mom: Well, that's you if you want to think stupid like that.

Marlon: (**approaches bouncing a ball**) Dude, I know I didn't just hear you say Daddy! How many times do I have to tell you we ain't got no Daddy!!

Mom: Ha! Shut up End of discussion.

QT: Marlon, we do man. Whether you want to acknowledge it or not we have one. And furthermore, you should be trying to take care of your responsibilities and be a daddy to the child you have coming into the world so he or she won't end up like us!!

Mom: Marlon, have you gone and gotten some girl pregnant? Is you crazy? Oh my God, don't y'all ever think about everything I have to deal with now.

Marlon: Ma, its cool...that girl ain't nothing!! Besides I'm not the only guy that done slept with her so I know I'm not the daddy. I wrapped up and I'm too young to have kids anyways. QT, I'm fine with who I am...A player...always have been and always will be!! I don't care about these girls or who they say they're pregnant by. She should have taken a pill or something...I ain't trying to be no daddy-not now or not ever! (**Walks away**)

Mom: Shut up and get back here, Marlon cause you sounding real stupid right now. Didn't you learn about using condoms in health class, and age doesn't have anything to do with having a child. Uggghh, you sound just like your stupid daddy when you said that.

Marlon: Yes, ma, I used one so, that's another reason why I KNOW I'M NOT THE FATHER!

Mom: Condoms are not always secure, stupid! Uh… God! I'm going to bed. I can't deal with this right now (**walks out going to bed**)

Marlon: I'm going to my room to listen to Round of Applause (baby make that a** clap) singing as he walks away

QT: Ma!!! Marlon!! Wait!! Ma, can't we just talk about this?

MOM: There's nothing to talk about. I'm done with it, now everybody just leave me alone.

Marlon: Sounds good to me, ma! QT, find some sense, bruh. We don't have a daddy just like Keisha baby won't have a daddy. It's just life, bro. Deal with it!

(QT walks around the room frustrated, sees a bottle of pills and takes all of them, starts to stumble and falls out on the floor)

QT: I'll just end all of my hurt right now! I'm worthless anyway

(**The mother walks in and finds her son of the floor**)

Mom: (pulling him off the floor) QT? QT? QT? Oh God, what have you done? Why, Lord, Why? (Screams for Marlon) Marlon, Marlon, call 911, call 911! Hurry, hurry! Oh God, oh God, oh my Jesus (**the mother is crying and screaming**)

(QT is rushed to the hospital)

(Mom and Marlon make it to the hospital and they are constantly praying that QT lives.)

Scene 6

Narrator- We have to listen to the whispers before our kids start screaming.

**Today is the day of the book signing for "Sista Let Me Tell Ya, Bruh If You Only Knew"……
Let's listen in on this extraordinary event….**

Author: We've got to start listening to the whispers of our children before they start screaming! Our kids have been whispering, but we are too tired to listen. Our kids are whispering, but we would rather sleep. Can I tell you something for free? We've got teenage girls thinking their bodies are money-making mechanisms. This is the result of the Willie Lynch letter that was written in 1712. Isn't it funny how something can affect you even though you never knew it existed? Isn't it funny how two pages in a letter has caused all this damage to the family (**drops the two pages on the floor and walks away**)

(QT walks out while all the other characters are on the stage talking. When he begins to speak each character is frozen until time for them to speak)

QT: No one was there to listen to my whispers and in the next three months I will have had 4 suicidal attempts and the last one was successful (**freezes after he speaks**)

Kesha: I had an abortion. I couldn't deal with trying to raise a child on my own when I'm only a child. I don't understand….all I really wanted was for someone to love me. I thought that sex was the best way to receive love from a guy. I never really learned my lesson. I've had three abortions, total and I'm pregnant right now…I don't know how this one will end up, but I'm hoping this guy really loves me (**freezes after she speaks**)

Jessica: I went on to pursue my dreams to become the first family member to go to college. I had some struggles in life, but I'm proud to say that I'm the first family member to break the cycle in my family. I live in Atlanta, GA and I'm proud to say that I'm a successful pediatrician (**freezes after she speaks**)

Marlon: I'm still a player, still a pimp, and still don't care about NOTHING OR NOBOBY! Do you know how many women I have under my belt now? So many I can't even count!! Funny thing is, I leave a little something for them to remember me by each and every time I leave them and it's called AIDS!! Yeah, you heard me…AIDS. After all my playing….guess I'm the one that really got played, huh? (**freezes after he speaks**)

Mom: I guess I could have taken the time out to really talk to my sons, let them know how much I loved them, but how could I?! I mean, I had to balance work, choir rehearsal, keeping food on the table, and being a single mom. I, I, I tried but I just didn't know how!! Heck, I didn't get the love I needed when I was young either, so I really didn't know how to give it!! Now, I have one in the grave and one on the way there. Now, I find myself with nothing but time to think about what I could have done! (**freezes after she speaks**)

Cindy: After being touched by a powerful message that the author shared at the book signing that day, I decided to go to college and become a lawyer. I found out it's not about BET or music videos, even tho that's what I really enjoyed doing. I'm doing so much more with a degree (**freezes after she speaks**)

Christopher: I went to college and became a doctor and a youth minister. I finally got the guts to propose to Cindy and we got married after College. In the beginning, QT called me a nerd, but I guess the nerd still had the most SWAG (**freezes after he speaks**)

Author: I traveled the world spreading my message. Sometimes, there were few and sometimes there were many. But everywhere I went....I touched a life (**freezes after he speaks**)

Narrator- "Sista let me tell ya, Bruh if you only knew"

1. As you were reading the play, which scene impacted you the most?

   _____
   _____
   _____
   _____
   _____

2. Which character could you identify with the most from the play? What characteristics did you and the character have in common? Were those traits negative or positive? If they were negative, what can you do to change them?

   _____
   _____
   _____
   _____

3. Which character were you the most disappointed with and why?

   _____
   _____
   _____
   _____

4. What impact did scene 6 have on you as an individual? What can we do as a society to change the outcome of what happened in scene 6 from occurring in the future?

   _____
   _____
   _____
   _____

Chapter Seven Reflections

"If you leave and grow, you can comeback and plant."
Marquis Cooper, Sr.

Thoughts to Remember

❖ Start now by being **P**repared, **M**otivated, and **D**estined to become successful. Daily apply the 15 principles in chapter seven… **(PMD)**

❖ **W**atch the people that want you to make it, **L**earn from those that don't want you to make it, and **O**bserve everyone in between (including yourself); then you can **G**o expecting, **G**et what you came for, and **L**eave smiling…. **(WLO so you can GGL)**

Question to Consider

❖ Are you ready to leave and grow, so that you can come back and plant?

Point to Ponder

❖ William Lynch provided principles to destroy and break a certain race of people (African Americans). His principles somehow crossed racial lines creating dysfunctional families which tainted the male/female images among ALL races. Lynch mentioned that ONLY a phenomenal shift would restore the natural order. That shift is taking place NOW, and simple guidelines have been outlined within the pages of this workbook. The time for change is NOW, the time for action is NOW, the time to close the communication gap is NOW!!!

Quote to Carry

❖ "It is far easier to build strong children than it is to repair broken men"- Frederick Douglass

Please take a moment to answer the following questions about the R.E.N.E.W. program

1. What impact has this curriculum had on you? Have you benefited from coming to the weekly sessions? If so, how?

   _____

   _____

   _____

   _____

   _____

   _____

2. How did you see yourself before you started the R.E.N.E.W. curriculum compared to how you see yourself now? Have you changed in a major way? If so, how?

   _____

   _____

   _____

   _____

   _____

   _____

3. Do you think other students would benefit from going through the R.E.N.E.W. curriculum? Do you think parents and educators would benefit as well? Explain your answers thoroughly

   _____

   _____

   _____

   _____

   _____

   _____

   _____

   _____

   _____

   _____

Thank you for taking time to read the book and to complete the workbook activities. At this time, I ask that you provide additional comments on the material. Please use the space below to share your thoughts with your teacher/facilitator. Be sure to hand this in at the end of the session. Please be completely honest because your reflections may be shared with others in the near future. Be sure to include your name, school, and city and state. The evaluation may be mailed to the address found in the back of the book.

EVALUATION

_____
_____
_____
_____
_____
_____
_____
_____
_____
_____
_____
_____
_____
_____
_____
_____
_____
_____
_____
_____
_____
_____
_____

Tips for Graduating Seniors

In an effort to empower and motivate this generation of future leaders, here are 15 tips that graduating seniors can apply to their everyday life. These tips will ensure you are prepared, motivated, and destined for your journey through college and for a successful life.

Tip #1

Don't get comfortable once you receive your high school diploma. Once you walk across the platform the spirit of complacency must cease to exist in your life. You must surround yourself with positive people that are doing positive things that are determined to go positive places in life.

Tip #2

Don't allow other people to dictate your future. Your level of success will be determined by the daily effort you contribute to it. You will soon learn you can't look for people to validate your success. If a person can't validate who they are internally, then there's no way possible for them to validate you externally.

Tip #3

Start decreasing your dependency on other people, and learn to tap into the inner strengths you didn't know you possessed. You will become who you are destined to become without receiving validation from anyone. The key to survival is being meticulous with whom you allow to speak into your life. Remember, some people will not be willing to help you because they fear the strength you possess.

Tip #4

Become more assertive in making your dreams a reality starting today. For the past 18 years others have spoke for you, woke you up so you wouldn't oversleep, and covered you in every direction. Freedom awaits you but just remember, "Freedom without control can be dangerous".

Tip #5

If you plan to attend college tomorrow you must change your mind set today. One of the biggest keys to being successful in college is to build strong working relationships with your professors. Sometimes the key to mastering personalities will unlock the door to mastering subjects.

Tip #6

Don't allow your weakness to dictate your future. In life you will encounter many obstacles which seem insurmountable, but you must possess a GGL attitude to overcome this feeling of self defeat. GGL simply means to: <u>G</u>o expecting, <u>G</u>et what you came for, and <u>L</u>eave smiling.

Tip #7

Hold on to the level of excitement you will experience once your name is called out. In times when life gets difficult, simply reflect on the applause you heard the day you received your diploma. The ultimate challenge is how to stay motivated when no one is cheering for you.

Tip #8

Learn how to speak into your own spirit and encourage yourself at times. A lot of the people that saw you through are now depending on you to one day come back and see them through. Every day will not be a good day, but each day will become what you make of it.

Tip #9

Understand that each day brings new challenges. Once you leave the covering of high school, you will face the challenges of life. Don't quit because things are difficult, keep pushing until you reach your destined place in life.

Tip #10

Understand early and often that some of your friends can't go where destiny is going to take you. The truth of the matter is they can't go with you because their mentality will not allow them to go. Don't allow anyone to hold you back from what you were created to do. The worst part about life is waking up every day with a lot of what If's.

Tip #11

Realize from this day forward you will be battling to reach your purpose in life. You must understand that arriving at your destined place not only affects you, it affects those who see you as an example. Some people are waiting on you to arrive in life so they can start their journey in life.

Tip #12

Learn to shut the door on all distractions. Distractions come in different forms but they serve a common purpose, and that is to keep you from your destined place in life. The quicker you identify the distracter, the quicker you can stop being distracted. In every area of your life you will find some distracters, just make sure that the distracter is not YOU.

Tip #13

Recondition the mind to reinvent all prior successes in life. Many graduates never arrive at their destined place in life because they failed to hold on to things that helped them achieve in life. EX: If you received awards or any type of positive recognition during your tenure through high school, take those awards with you to college as a reminder of what you're capable of achieving through hard work and dedication.

Tip #14

Forget about where you are in order to get to where you're going. In other words, recognize and let go of whatever it is in your past that is holding you back from the present, and preventing you from obtaining a successful future.

Tip #15

In school you learned to recite the pledge of allegiance, but before going off to college you must learn the WLO allegiance. WLO seems very elementary, but in essence it's a life changing phrase if you apply it to your everyday life. **WATCH** the people that want you to make it. **LEARN** from those that don't want you to make it. **OBSERVE** everyone in between (including yourself).

In closing, one of the keys to life is being able to give back to your community once you become successful in life. If you the reader will make a commitment to yourself and these 15 tips there is nothing in life that you cannot achieve. Whatever you do in life just remember these words, "If you leave and grow, you can come back and plant"- Marquis Cooper.

Note: These 15 tips can also be found in Chapter 7 of "Sista let me tell ya, bruh if you only knew, Real talk for Parents and Educators, From Me to You".

APPENDIX A

R.E.N.E.W. (Removing Every Negative Emotion and Word)
Sample Questionnaire Data

My greatest struggle is (a struggle is defined as something you changed about yourself)

- My attitude, character, and how I see myself
- Attitude, music, peer pressure, and anger
- Helping others more than helping myself
- How to have a greater relationship with God
- Doing the right thing
- I don't have one

If there was one thing I could change about myself it would be the way I (Ex, the way I think, the way I act, play to much etc…)

- How I feel toward myself, my personality, and my attitude
- Approaching bad situations because I laugh at everything
- Letting everything get to me
- Choose friends
- Stop playing when it's time to be serious
- Be a little more thankful for the things I have

This is one question I would like to discuss during our RENEW sessions

- Helping our community make better decisions
- Why do people think that men are unfaithful
- Why do black men abandon their children

What is one question you have always wanted to ask someone (adult) but never had the courage to do so?

- Am I ugly?
- Why do adults hide the hurt they have but expect us to share what we are feeling?
- Why do parents stress you out?
- Why do adults SAG?
- WHY CANT I ASK WHY?

APPENDIX B

R.E.N.E.W. (Removing Every Negative Emotion and Word)
Post student Questionnaire

PLEASE PUT YOUR NAME ON THIS FORM

Grade_____ Age_____ School_____ Sex M_____ F_____

My greatest struggle was (**a struggle is defined as something you want to change about yourself but just don't know how**)

_____

_____

_____

_____

The one thing I changed about myself was the way I (**Ex: the way I thought**)

_____

_____

_____

_____

This is one question that was an answered for me during our weekly R.E.N.E.W. sessions (**Ex: Why won't you explain yourself?**)

_____

_____

_____

_____

This is one question I was finally able to ask an adult (**Ex: Why are grownups so serious all the time?**)

_____

_____

_____

_____

APPENDIX C

Sample Partnership Letter for R.E.N.E.W.

Date: _____

To Whom It May Concern:

My name is _____. I am the facilitator of the R.E.N.E.W. program here at _____. I am in the process of trying to partner with various organizations to help sponsor a young lady that's involved in the R.E.N.E.W. (Removing Every Negative Emotion & Word) program here at _____. There are many people that talk about the negativity facing our teenage females, but in reality if we would begin to offer a more positive avenue, then our girls would follow suit. I am asking if your organization would partner with _____ and be that beacon of light for our young ladies. The only commitment that's needed is to come and share with the young ladies on any First Friday afternoon of any month during the year.

The purposes of the meetings are three-fold: 1) to help close the communication gap among parents, students, and educators, 2) to create cultural awareness of how the past affects the future, and 3) to shed light on your personal struggle (s) toward success. I hope after reading this letter your organization will be willing to help change the condition and the mentality of our young ladies here at _____. If you need to contact me I can be reached at _____ or you can email me at _____.
I look forward to hearing from someone regarding this proposition, and I want to thank you in advance for your time.

I will end with a quote by Frederick Douglass that states, "It is far easier to build strong children, than it is to repair broken men (women)".

Respectfully,

APPENDIX D

Sample Partnership Letter for R.E.N.E.W.

Date: _____

To Whom It May Concern:

My name is _____. I am the facilitator of the R.E.N.E.W. program here at _____. I am in the process of trying to partner with various organizations to help sponsor a young man that's involved in the R.E.N.E.W. (Removing Every Negative Emotion & Word) program here at _____. There are many people that talk about the negativity facing our teenage males, but in reality if we would begin to offer a more positive avenue, then our males would follow suit. I am asking if your organization would partner with _____ and be that beacon of light for our young men. The only commitment that's needed is to come and share with the young men on any third Friday afternoon of any month during the year.

The purposes of the meetings are three-fold: 1) to help close the communication gap among parents, students, and educators, 2) to create cultural awareness of how the past affects the future, and 3) to shed light on your personal struggle (s) toward success. I hope after reading this letter your organization will be willing to help change the condition and the mentality of our young men here at _____. If you need to contact me I can be reached at _____ or you can email me at _____. I look forward to hearing from someone regarding this proposition, and I want to thank you in advance for your time.

I will end with a quote by Frederick Douglass that states, "It is far easier to build strong children, than it is to repair broken men (women)".

Respectfully,

Real Talk from Me to You

Marquis Cooper, Sr. M. Ed (ABD

How we can we save our black young men has been the discussion that has taken place in schools, churches, community centers, and other venues across this country for years. As a school counselor, I understand the many challenges that our black males are faced with each and every day. I also believe there is a solution to a problem that seems to be out of control. I was born and raised in a small town in Eastern Arkansas called Marianna, Arkansas. I grew up in a blended family, which means a family that is formed when separate families are united by marriage. My mother bore 12 children during her first marriage, and my father had 9 children during his first marriage. The story goes, when my siblings found out that my mother was pregnant with me, they all told her that the only thing she needed to bring home was a cat. Needless to say, I became the 22ⁿᵈ child which completed my family. I'm the only child they had together, so for the most part I considered myself to be an only child because I grew up without the rest of the "football" team.

Growing up in Marianna at one point and time was a city to be proud of, but during the late 80's the image of the town slowly begin to fall apart. The story of the Chambers brothers, (leaders of a Marianna to Detroit crack cocaine connection), created a dark shadow that the city has never been able to live down. Some people believed that if you were from Marianna, then your fate rested in being a thug, murderer, criminal, or drug dealer. Recently, Marianna once again became the focus of negative media attention following the stories of Curtis Vance, (convicted of killing KATV anchorwoman Ann Presley), Maurice Clemmons, (killed by police who sought him for the shooting deaths of four police officers in Washington State), and now Operation Delta blues (a major drug raid that netted 70 indictments). The sad reality is most of the aforementioned stories were all connected to black males, which further validated the point that something must be done if we are going to stop this vicious cycle.

In 2009 the U.S. Census Bureau did a study on the number of single parents and the amount of child support they received (does not represent all single parents).[2] The bureau reported that there was an estimated 13.7 million single parents who had custody of 21.8 million children age 21 and under. Mothers accounted for 82.6% and fathers accounted for 17.4%. Yes, that is true. The results prove that we have more single women raising children alone. The numbers don't lie. There are very few positive male role models in the home to set an example.

At some point in history, we created this seed of irresponsibility in our males. As a result, the prison system is overpopulated and we have done nothing to change the outcome. I believe there is something we can do to reclaim our males, and it starts with re shifting the male into his proper position in the household.

Please allow me to paint a picture and make it clear. The standard order for a "two" parent household is that of the father, wife, son and daughter. A plan was devised many years ago that changed the structure of the family, especially the positioning of the male. In many African American homes across this country the family structure looks like the following: You have the son (in an unknown spot), mother (in the father's spot), daughter (behind her mother out of her spot), and the father (totally removed from the family he has no spot). Here is an illustration for those of you who are visual learners; please read from left to right.

Normal Family Structure	Father (head of house)	Wife (beside the head)	Son (beside the mother)	Daughter (beside the brother)
Son (positioned beside his mom on left side)	Wife (positioned where the father was)	Daughter (positioned behind her mom)	Father (positioned nowhere)	Dysfunctional Family Structure

When this style of familial transfer takes charge, it has a profound effect on the entire family unit, but more so with the male. The African American male population has been far more effected

---

2   Grall, Timothy, US Census Bureau, *Custodial Mothers and Fathers and their Child Support: 2007.* (updated 2008 April; sited 2010 March 6) available from: http://www.census.gov/prod/2009pubs/p60-237.pdf

than any other ethnic group. The African American population is only 13.5% of the American population.[3] The crucial problem that has now arisen is how to change a family structure that has been perfected in the life of the African American male for the past 300 years.

The crisis for the black male occupying an unknown spot has created a major crisis within the black community. This crisis can be seen in most homes, neighborhoods, schools, college campuses, and even on jobs. What is the crisis you might ask? The crisis as it relates to the men in America looks like this:

> *a nation of pant **sagging**, interchangeable grill mouth **wearing**, bling bling **wanting**, big rims **seeking**, foul language **using**, sports driven **dreamers**, fashion statement **makers**, non vision **having**, no purpose in life **wanting**, silly acting **daily**, non identity **having**, name **seekers**.*

The above scenario exists because "the man is out of place, the woman is displaced, and the children have become misplaced "–Marquis Cooper. The good news is there's still hope to change the fate of many black males in America. We can no longer allow 72% of our black males to fail in life because their father chose not to be in their lives. We can no longer allow the aforementioned crisis; I shared in the above paragraph to continue to be the "norm" for black males. We can no longer make excuses for not reaching back to save our young black males.

The plight of the African American male in society seems to be getting worse by the minute. A lot of young men have no lamp (father) to observe, and they are being guided by the light (mother) only. A light (mother) without a lamp (father) is dangerous. A lot of young black males have no idea of what it takes to be a good leader because they've never seen one. Tupac echoes this message in his song "Keep Ya Head Up" from his Still I Rise album. He states, "Say there ain't no hope for the youth and the truth is it ain't no hope for tha future". I have to agree whole heartedly with Tupac because if we believe there is no hope for the youth, then we are doomed. There is hope to save this generation of young black males, but it all starts with knowing, believing, and internalizing the power of It's OK.

The circle of change for our black males in our homes, schools, and communities begins with knowing the power of "It's OK." So my fellow males, I want you to know that's "It's Ok" to be intelligent. "It's OK," to break and lead at the same time. "It's OK," not to use slang every time you speak. "It's OK" to speak correct English. "It's OK," if you do not want to play sports. "It's OK," to keep your pants up and not sag. "It's OK," if you don't want rims on your car. "It's OK," if you don't want to act silly while in class. "It's OK," for you to open the door anytime a lady is present. "It's OK" to be respectful at all times. "It's OK," to shake a young ladies hand and say goodnight. "It's OK," for you to use your manners. "It's OK," for you to clean up your room. "It's OK," to vacuum the house. "It's OK" to be a leader. "It's OK" not to use profanity. "It's OK" to have a vision in life. "It's OK" to know your purpose in life. Most importantly "It's OK" to be you.

Through the power of "It's OK," we can save the lives of countless black males in this generation. Frederick Douglass states, "It is far easier to build strong children than to repair broken men". I believe what Frederick Douglass stated years ago, the question is do you?

---

3   U S Census Bureau, African Americans by the numbers. (Updated 2008 July 1: sited 2010 March 6) http://www.infoplease.com/spot/bhmcensus1.html

Cooper, M. (2010). Sista let me tell ya, Bruh if you only knew, Real talk for Parents and Educators, From Me to You. Indiana: Author house.

Real Talk from Me to You

Marquis Cooper, Sr. M. Ed (ABD)

One of the greatest disconnects we currently face in the 21st century is a language barrier. We speak a different language than that of our children. Parents, how many of you will agree there are times when you are clueless of the things your child is going through in life. How many of you will agree there are times when you feel like you are making progress only to find out you really aren't. How many of you will agree that your child spends more time texting, talking to their friends, and time on face book than they do anything else. If you feel this way, you are not alone because many parents feel this way. The problem with this generation compared to any other generation is that our youth have an appreciation for noise, while past generations have an appreciation for sound. I know you may have thought that noise and sound were the same, but contrary to popular belief, they are very different.

According to Webster Dictionary, sound is defined as free from error, whole, stable, healthy, rational, or valid.[4] On the other hand, noise is defined as loud, confused, senseless, shouting, unwanted, undesired, or unpleasant.[5] I want to ensure you that these two words are not the same. As parents, the problem we face on a daily basis is how to reach a generation that has confused "sound" with "noise." I want to be very candid and help parents understand the phrase, "do as I say and not as I do", does not carry the same influence it once did. If truth be told, it really didn't affect previous generations as much as we would like to think it did. What impacted previous generations was having a solid family structure which reinforced the principles echoed through those words.

One of the easiest ways to find out where you are as it relates to this generation is to test your knowledge on the problems we are currently experiencing throughout this country. Allow me to share a simple exercise to help you understand the language barrier which exists with our youth. One of my biggest beliefs is that we are losing our children on a daily basis because we have no idea of the language they are speaking. Whether you choose to accept it or not, the music your child listens to can have a substantial influence on whom they become.

As a parent and educator, I pride myself on being connected to the system of entertainment that is profoundly influencing our children. This exercise is only meant to enlighten you, and make you more aware of things you may not have known. As parents, if we are not speaking enough of our children's language then the sad reality is we may be losing them. Below is a short exercise to see how well you know what your children are listening to. The only thing I ask of you is remain honest and do not ask for help while completing this short quiz.

Directions: Match the correct artist with the correct song.

1. **I just call her boo**	a. **Plies**
2. **Make me proud**	b. **Jeremiah**
3. **Goin Steady**	c. **Yo Gotti**
4. **Round of Applause**	d. **Drake**
5. **Swag On**	e. **Wacka Floka**
6. **Birthday Sex**	f. **Soulja Boy**
7. **5 Star Chic**	g. **Shawty Putt**
8. **Becky**	h. **Tity Boi**
9. **Dat Baby Don't Look Like Me**	i. **Rocko**
10. **Invented Sex**	j. **Trey Songz**

As you completed this exercise, did you feel helpless? Did you feel like you were out of touch with reality? Did you feel like you were on the Maury show while trying to figure out one of the songs? Did you ever feel like you needed help from someone? Did you ever feel like giving up because you did not know the answers? The logic behind this exercise was to allow the reader to understand the difficulty that may arise when you are communicating with your child. If you answered no to most of these questions don't feel bad because this exercise was only done to show you one of the reasons why communication is so difficult.

---

4   Webster, "Sound." 137
5   Webster, "Noise." 137

As parents, we must begin to open the door of communication with our children. Many times we believe it is not necessary for our children to know about our life's struggles, disappointments, hardships, setbacks, and major pitfalls. I have come to the realization that there are some similarities in how teenagers view their parents, in relation to how parents view their children. Please understand communication does create an environment for exposure. The more time you communicate the more can reveal about who you really are. Most children want to open up to their parents, but because of the communication restraint they choose not to. Parents the communication restraint must cease, and it must stop after you finish reading this article. We must be real with our children about past circumstances and situations. It is only through the sharing of your story that your sons and daughters will be able to share their stories.

The Cherokee Proverb, "If you listen to the whispers, you won't have to hear the screams," is the mere basis behind the writing of this article. Parents we can no longer allow our children to call our names and we not answer. We can no longer tell our children to go somewhere else and not expect them to end up somewhere else. We can no longer allow the whisper of our children to go unattended. We can no longer ignore the whisper and not expect to hear the scream. The time to close the communication gap is NOW!!!

Cooper, M. (2010). Sista let me tell ya, Bruh if you only knew, Real talk for Parents and Educators, From Me to You. Indiana: Author house.

Author's Corner

Marquis Cooper, Sr. is a 1994 graduate of Lee High School in Marianna, AR. He obtained the following degrees: a Bachelor of Arts degree from Philander Smith College, a Master's degree in counseling from the University of Arkansas at Little Rock, and is currently writing his dissertation to attain his Doctorate in Educational Administration at the University of Arkansas at Little Rock. He is a licensed counselor for grades K-12 in the states of Tennessee and Arkansas.

Since 1996 he has served as an advocate for children at the elementary, middle, and high school levels. In 2009 he was chosen to be the school counselor at Star Academy which was a dropout prevention/credit recovery program for students in the Pulaski County Special School District. This program was the first of its kind in the state of Arkansas. Currently, he serves as the 9th grade school counselor at Maumelle High School in the Pulaski County Special School District.

Cooper is an accomplished educator. He has graced the stage of audiences in Arkansas, Indianapolis, Tennessee, and Texas where he has presented jaw dropping presentations focusing solely on character enhancement. Aside from his educational duties for the school systems, Cooper also put efforts in place to reach youth in his hometown. He is the President of the "Our Story" Youth Leadership Conference. This is an annual event that takes place in his hometown of Marianna, Arkansas each year. Our Story is for former graduates to reunite each year to impact the lives of children, parents, and educators in the community. Our Story was recognized by the Character Education Partnership as a National Promising Practice for 2012.

Cooper wrote and published Guidance ~N~ Action in 2008 which is recognized as a Model program for the National Dropout Prevention Center. In the wake of all of Cooper's hard work and dedication he took time to unleash the secrets and behaviors that are experienced by families. *Sista let me tell ya, Bruh if you only knew, Real Talk for Parents and Educators, From Me to You* was released August 2010. The book was recognized as one of the "Top 100 books of 2010" by Conversations Live Magazine.

He coined the phrase, "If you leave and grow, you can come back and plant." He continues to plant seeds of success and instill change by helping others to understand that their current circumstance does not dictate their future. Marquis is the youngest of 22 children in his family. He is a proud husband and father of Marquis Jr. and Cobie Cooper. Cooper currently resides in Little Rock, AR and serves as the youth minister at Greater Center Star M.B. Church.

15 QUOTES TO LIVE BY

"Just because you're surrounded by folks doesn't mean you are surrounded by followers"- Marquis Cooper, Sr.

"It is far easier to build strong children than to repair broken men"- Frederick Douglass

"Doubt and fear from your past can derail you from being successful in the future"- Marquis Cooper, Sr.

"History repeats itself because no one was listening the first time"- Unknown author

A lot of young men now have no LAMP (father) to observe and they are being guided by the LIGHT (mother) only. A LIGHT (mother) without a LAMP (father) is dangerous- Marquis Cooper, Sr.

"Sometimes in life you have to remove yourself (get rid of distractions) so you can see yourself"- Marquis Cooper, Sr.

"Why would someone be envious of you when you don't have what they have? It's because they know in due season you will have more than what they have"- Marquis Cooper, Sr.

"If you leave and grow you can come back and plant"- Marquis Cooper, Sr.

"If you listen to the whispers, you won't have to hear the screams"- Cherokee Proverb

"The past holds the key to the present, and the present holds access to the future"- Marquis Cooper, Sr.

"When the man is out of place, the woman becomes displaced, and the children become misplaced"- Marquis Cooper, Sr.

"When your present is not in order, your future is in danger of being chaotic"- Marquis Cooper, Sr.

"A secure leader will put you out front, a scared leader will put you behind, and an insecure leader will put you out"- Marquis Cooper, Sr.

"As a leader if you have someone under you who's shining don't be afraid to put them out front because their shine will make you look radiant"- Marquis Cooper, Sr.

"You see things and you say why, but I see things that never were and I say why not"- George Bernard Shaw

OTHER BOOKS BY MARQUIS COOPER, SR.

Guidance ~N~ Action is preparation endowed with an infinite affiliation for success. This curriculum was written for school counselors who work with students grades K-8. This program is designed to cultivate the traditional stance of public school life to an elevated advancement that involves closing the gap between the children that are "celebrated" and those that are "tolerated". Children often times steer where they stare, however with proper guidance imparted they can be groomed into being responsible, well rounded adults. Moreover, the vision entails the conception of liberation for every child to push past their immediate environment to reach the climax of possibilities for tomorrow. The program is patterned to transform dreams into reality with the energetic concept of GGL (**Go** expecting, **Get** what you came for, and **Leave** Smiling). Guidance ~N~ Action was recognized as a model program on the National Dropout Prevention website in late 2010.

The words are so profound and timely and relevant to people of ALL ages and backgrounds. The flow of the book is spot on. The opening chapter sets an enthralling tone for the rest of the book. It reminds us "Ignorance is NOT bliss, it's simply Ignorance". I can't imagine families NOT reading this book together. It is a MUST read for book clubs, youth groups, parents, pastors, educators, and etc. The book has a vernacular that is REAL and easy to understand on all level. This message will change and enlighten the lives of both students and educators and will reverse some of the unique challenges that African American students are faced with throughout the nation. The book wasn't just written for African Americans, but was written with all ethnicities in mind.

TO CONTACT THE AUTHOR PLEASE WRITE, EMAIL, OR CALL:

Marquis L. Cooper, Sr.
P.O. Box 30392
Little Rock, Arkansas 72260
SBRF@att.net or Cooper3471@aol.com
www.listentothewhispers.org and www.thevolarmag.com

1-901-786-2322

Endnotes

Paper Back:
Lynch, Willie *The Willie Lynch Letter and the Making of A Slave*. Snowball Publishing, 2009. 48pp. Print

Lynch, 62

Lynch, 64

Lynch, 69

2 Kopp

The New Sexual Revolution Is Here. (sited 2012 May 31) http://www.chastity.com/chastity-qa/stds/stds/sexual-exposure-chart/sexual-exposure-

Jones, L.J. (1995). The future of the family. New York: Prentice Hall

About the Authors

Marquis Cooper, S., M. Ed (ABD)

Marquis Cooper, Sr. has spent the past 14 years as a public school educator. He presently serves as the 9th grade counselor at Maumelle High School in the Pulaski County Special School District. He is an award winning educator, author of two books, and a nationally renowned motivational speaker. Mr. Cooper is a highly sought after speaker at both the local and national level. He is President of "Our Story" Youth Leadership Organization in Marianna, AR. This nonprofit organization began in 2010, and to date has created a platform for 27 former graduates to return and plant into the community. "Our Story" was recognized by the Character Education Partnership as a National Promising Practice for 2012. Mr. Cooper coined the phrase, "If you leave and grow, you can come back and plant." As an educator, he continues to plant seeds of success and instill change by helping youth to understand that their current circumstance does not dictate their future.

Tina Duffy

Adriaka "Tina" Duffy is the founder and President of *Grace and Mercy Center of Hope* (GMCH) which centers on being a positive influence in the lives of youth in her community. In 2009, she developed and launched the teen/young adult ministry, Y.E.E.S (*Youth at Emmaus Empowered to Serve*); and the college ministry, P.R.E.S.S (*Promoting, Reinforcing, and Encouraging Student Success*), at Emmaus Christian Church in Indianapolis, IN. Tina joined forces with her childhood friend, Marquis Cooper, Sr., as he launched his book *"Sista Let Me Tell Ya, Bruh If You Only Knew, Real Talk for Parents and Educators from Me to You."* She is currently implementing the R.E.N.E.W program in Indianapolis, IN.